KU-338-869

Foreword

Trucking, for me, is a combination of the very best and the very worst of jobs. I have

been to places and seen things that the average man in the street could not even imagine.

Sunrise over the mountains in Salzburg, reflecting in the lake, bringing me to tears at its

phenomenal natural beauty. Swiss-style chalets in Aosta in Northern Italy lit up with fairy

lights in the very early hours of Christmas Eve, twinkling and sparkling in the snow-rimed

landscape. Vast swathes of vineyards in the southern French villages, being lovingly tended

by black-dressed elderly women, whilst men in the background sit in the sun, drinking wine.

Without the HGV licence I would probably never have had the chance to observe and enjoy

such sights. There has been comedy, there have been tears, but only very seldom has there

been boredom.

The downside is that it really is a job for a single man. Marriages and other

relationships so frequently do not last, which is why I refer to 'Girlfriend du jour' throughout.

I am not a prodigiously romantic person, but I discovered that a relationship is so often not

sustainable when time and distance are thrown into the mix. You can easily be away from

home for six months at a time, and it is simply unfair on the partner who has to stay at home

and keep house.

It has to be said, though, that in the midst of beauty there can be chaos. One of the

pre-requisites of good continental truck drivers is the ability to think on their feet, or

technically on their arse, because there are no plans so carefully made, no schedules so pains-

takingly drawn up that the hand of Murphy cannot totally screw up with just a little prod.

What follows is, in itself, a journey. My journey, from disenchanted coach driver to a

member of the brotherhood (and increasingly sisterhood) of professional truck drivers. Next time you grow annoyed with the truck in front of you, just remember that he could be me.

Give them a wave and a smile. At the very least you will confuse them for the rest of the day!

Glossary

Before we embark on the journey, I should explain that I will be using technical terms throughout the book. I have, therefore, compiled a list of the more important terms for your information, and to save you scurrying for the dictionary. (I should point out that my concern is not so much that you should tire yourself in your relentless quest for knowledge and understanding, but that you should find the dictionary to be more entertaining than the book you are now reading)

Articulated Lorry:

A Heavy Goods unit designed to carry maximum volume and weight. These things are also designed to bend when turning. This can come as a bit of a surprise if you have just sneaked up the inside at a crossroads or similar intersection when the artic is clearly indicating a left turn and yet is sitting on the right hand side of the road. Clearly he has left his indicator on in error, right? Wrong... That will be because he needs to swing out to the right before he turns left. And the trailer that is currently on your right is shortly going to be collecting you and your car, and introducing it forcefully to the pavement, because, of course, you are now in the blind spot, and the truck driver cannot see you. If you happened to be the driver of the rather pretty pink VW Beetle in Winchester, well, now you know!

Artic:

Another term for Articulated Lorry. See also HGV

Arctic:

When applied to geography, the most northerly part of the planet Earth. Not, in any way, another term for Articulated Lorry.

Car transporter:

A vehicle designed so the driver can have a multi vehicle accident all on his own.

CMR forms:

Convention des Marchandises Routiers.

Paperwork to facilitate the total confusion of drivers, warehousemen and customs officials throughout Europe.

Customs and Excise:

Throughout the known world Customs officials work tirelessly. No one really knows why.

Diesel:

The fuel that most trucks run on. Actually, more correctly called DERV (Diesel Engine, Road Vehicles) this fuel is a very pale yellow, incredibly smelly and slippery. You do not want to get it on your shoes if you want to keep your head higher than your feet. Red diesel is sold as a fuel for heating, for agricultural tractors and is tax reduced. Whilst it works equally well in cars and lorries, for some reason the Customs and Excise folk get quite peeved when people use it for such purposes.

Diesel:

Favourite word of one of my transport managers. We even nicknamed him Diesel Dave, for his habit of saying, 'Diesel go there, then diesel go over there…'

Double manning:

The act of running one truck with two drivers, to allow more driving time, and to help with difficult loads.

Duple:

A company that built coach bodies onto Bedford chassis, gearbox and engine.

Exhaust brake:

A device that is elegantly simple in operation. On long descents you really don't want to keep using the brakes, as they can overheat and rapidly lose effect. An exhaust brake basically shoves a cork in the engine exhaust, turning it into a very powerful brake at the push of a button, and allowing you to control your descent without resorting too often to the main brakes.

Exhaust break:

The time you take out of the cab of the truck when your co-driver has had Brussels sprouts curry for dinner again…

Fifth wheel:

The mechanical linkage on a tractor unit that allows the trailer to be connected. You would be surprised, I think, at just how small the actual connecting pin is. Don't, I caution you, have a look, or you will never ever tailgate a truck again.

Handbrake:

Device to mechanically and pneumatically lock the brakes in the 'on position' on a vehicle.

Hand break:

The result of trying to catch a two hundred kilo pallet.

HGV:

Heavy Goods Vehicle. Also LGV, or Large goods vehicle. Requires a special driving licence to operate, and a close attention to record keeping.

Night Trunking:

It is often convenient to move goods and materials between sites during the night, when roads are clearer, and factories and warehouses are not at full capacity. The technique of moving a load from one depot to another, dropping the load, collecting a replacement and returning to your own depot.

RORO:

Roll On, Roll Off ferries. These ships have doors at bow and stern, so trucks can drive on at the docks and drive straight off at the other end, without having to reverse.

Rororo:

Your boat. Gently down the stream

SatNav:

A device which allows you to get hopelessly lost to an accuracy previously undreamed of.

Sheet:

Canvas and plastic covering, designed to both enclose and secure your load on a tilt trailer or a flatbed.

Sheet!:

Your reaction when you realise you have just delivered the goods that were destined for York to Alicante.

Suzie:

The name given to the air lines and electrical couplings linking a tractor unit to a trailer.

T Forms:

A set of paperwork that is required to be filled in by an agent, and stamped by Customs and Excise, to allow the passage of goods over borders.

Tea forms:

Chitty for a free cuppa.

Tacho or Tachograph.

Device for recording drivers' hours, waiting time (see weight limit) break taken and road speed. Often known as the 'Spy in the Cab.' When I drove for a living it took the form of a device that recorded all driving hours, work that was not driving and breaks, on a waxed disc. Every day you changed the disc for a new one, and you had to keep the old discs for inspection by the police and other authorities. When you use a tacho disc you have to put your name, the start location, end location, and start and finish mileages on them, in pen. These days they are being superseded by electronic devices that store digitally the same information. The words tacho and tachograph can be used for both the device and the recording medium.

TIR park:

It is not uncommon for vehicles travelling in a foreign country to finally clear customs not at the border but considerably inland of the border. To that end there are 'TIR' parks. Transport Internationale Routiers, where un-cleared truck and trailer loads have to park and where they may finally get customs clearance.

Trailer:

There are many types of HGV trailer.

- Tilt. This is a common, yet horribly unwieldy form of trailer. Very much like a frame tent, it has a steel skeleton that holds the canvas roof and sides, and has been designed so that you have to dismantle it to load pretty much anything. To dismantle it you have to remove the incredibly heavy, unwieldy canvas tilt sheet. Normally in the dark, in the rain, at 2am, on your own. To rebuild it you simply have to reverse the dismantling procedure. Except you have to somehow haul the sheet fifteen feet onto the roof, then get all the fiddly eyes to fit the hooks on the framework. Which they never do. Then you have to feed the security cable through all 150 hooks and eyes. In the dark. And the cable will *always* have one sharp strand of wire which will either snag or rip a chunk of skin off your hand. And once you have got the whole lot together, the loading foreman will say, 'Sorry Drive, we forgot this bit. It's the most important part of the load. Can we just pop it on the trailer?'

- Reefer. A refrigerated trailer. Using the same technology as a standard household fridge, but expanded to industrial scale, these trailers are common on the roads. They either have a diesel engine and compressor at the front or slung underneath the trailer, and can freeze the entire trailer to below -20 degrees. Some are designed so that different areas can be set to different temperatures, allowing the operator to carry frozen foods, chilled foods, such as fruit and veg, and ambient, such as clothing. If you get it wrong, of course, you can find yourself delivering 650 deep frozen The Little Mermaid costumes to The Disney Shop on the Champs Elyse in Paris. Yes, I did.

- Flat bed. Not so common these days, this is just as it sounds, a flat trailer. A very useful trailer, but it does require the operator to have a grounding in roping and sheeting, lest he should wish to explain to the local constabulary exactly why he found it necessary to deliver twenty tonnes of glass milk bottles to the Renault garage on that tight bend. No, I didn't.

- Taut, taughtliner or curtain-sider. These trailers are possibly the easiest to use, under most circumstances. They are constructed as a flat-bed trailer, with a metal framework holding canvas curtains, which are pulled closed to contain the load, and fastened tightly with ratchet straps. It is worth remembering, however, that the curtains on their own are not designed to secure the load. Which is why you may see some of these trailers with bulges in the side, as the top pallet of bricks tries to make a break for freedom.

- Box trailer. The second simplest construction, being basically a box on wheels. The loads enter and leave through the back doors. These trailers are most commonly used for palletised goods that can be manoeuvred by means of a pallet truck.

There are other types, such as skeleton trailers, trombone trailers and step frame. Just be aware that skeleton trailers seldom carry bones, trombone trailers are pretty much useless for carrying brass band instruments, and step frame trailers have a step in the frame.

Unit:

Another name for Tractor.

U nit:

You've just delivered the goods that were destined for Axminster to Alicante.

Weight limit:

The maximum weight of vehicle allowed along a certain route. This may be due to it being in a residential area, or possibly due to a narrow or weak bridge or similar structure.

Wait limit:

'Look, if you don't get this bloody trailer loaded pretty quick I'm pulling out of the line and going home!'

A journey of a thousand miles begins with the first stumble

How many of us can claim to have followed a childhood ambition to its realisation? As children we looked upon the future with wide eyes, and each of us tried to imagine what that future would hold. Each of us had some idea of what we wanted to be, and for the most part that dream changed as we got older, as we became interested in different things.

I was lucky. I remember one of my ambitions, lowly as it was, was to be a truck driver, just like my Uncle Roy. How well I remember standing gazing in awe at the Volvo F88 that he parked outside our house on the very few occasions he visited us. To me that Goliath was the epitome of cool, and he, as its driver, was the very King of the Road.

That ambition never left me. However, I was not to realise my dream until over twenty years later, by which time I had been a laboratory assistant for the construction industry, a land drainage engineer, a video library owner, an electronics installation engineer, an ambulance paramedic and a coach driver. All of the jobs provided a certain level of satisfaction, but none of them, apart from the paramedic, gave me the buzz of a job well done...

I woke up in hospital. I knew, without conscious thought that it was a hospital. I'd experienced more waking up in hospital than I really wanted, and could recognise the clues. Soft pillows. The distant beep of a monitor. Quiet coughing. The too bright, sterile looking light. The smell of disinfectant that almost but not quite masked the odour of boiled cabbage.

Okay, I was in hospital, check. Next, where did I hurt? On cue my arm and neck started to throb and grate. I attracted the attention of a nurse by sitting up and yelping, she came over and spoke, in French. Right, either the NHS was having serious staffing problems, or I was in France. Pain relief was organised, and I sat back in a comfortable fug, waiting for things to start to make sense. Explanations would, I knew, happen in their own time, and in any case the morphia made straight-line thinking impossible. The little birds and fairies were far too distracting.

As I was driving for a coach and holiday company at the time I was well looked after. During the afternoon one of the company tour guides, Bruce, turned up to see me. I should point out that all tour guides look the same. They may have long hair, or short. They could have massive moustaches or other facial topiary. Piercings were not uncommon, nor were scars, nor broken noses. With or without glasses, in their company uniform of blazers and light grey slacks, they were still somehow identical. The same was true of the men. I used to call then all Bruce, to save time.

Bruce told me what had happened. Apparently I'd been 'off shift' and asleep in the driver's rest compartment of the coach. Situated under the seats on the left hand side of the vehicle, this is a small compartment big enough for the spare driver to sleep in, and if he is flexible enough, to get changed in. We all referred to it as 'The Coffin,' although up until that moment I hadn't realised how apt the soubriquet was. As we'd rounded a corner a Spanish registered truck laden with sheet steel had come the other way, and a corner of the steel had struck the side of the coach, opening up the side like a tin opener. In doing so it had cut through 'The Coffin,' removed my pillow from under my head, and managed to compact the entire compartment into a space about half its width. I'd been trapped in there for about two hours, most of the time unconscious, so I had no memory of the events, before I'd been cut free. It seems I'd been incredibly lucky to get away with the injuries I'd sustained, as had the steel been a couple of inches higher it would have left the pillow where it was, and instead removed my head from my shoulders. As it was, my head had been rattled around like a pea in a can and I suffered a broken nose, badly damaged neck and a smashed wrist watch. I have no idea how…

I was in the hospital in France for five weeks before being transported home, and off work for another two months before starting back to work. I'd expressed an interest in not shipping out abroad for a while, as I was still a little shaken up, and so the company had given me an 'easy' job to start back on. I had to transport a coach-load of scouts and cubs to Devon, in the oldest coach in the fleet, an ancient Duple-bodied Bedford. This, at least, should have been a piece of cake.

The first indication that this was not going to involve cake of any sort occurred at a rest break outside Glastonbury. We'd stopped at a grassy picnic area, and the cubs were having sandwiches and drinks, and running around being children. One of them then decided that what he really wanted to do was to slide down the grassy bank, which would have been fun were it not for the broken beer bottle hidden in the grass. The resultant wound required hospital treatment, so we all piled in to the coach and I drove around Glastonbury until we found the hospital. The unfortunate child was decanted, along with one of the supervisors, whilst I waited with the coach on the road outside.

The duo returned about an hour later, with the cub looking somewhat green. Apparently the cut to his buttock had required cleaning and stitching, and a number of injections of local anaesthetic had been applied round the area before this could take place. On top of this he'd been given antibiotics and oral painkiller. All of this, combined with fizzy drink and sweets, was not sitting well with him, and so he was given a seat at the front, behind the driver, with the supervisor.

Off we set, en-route to Devon. The road out of Glastonbury was long, straight and narrow, with reed beds either side. Before long I'd accumulated quite a queue of traffic behind me, as the Bedford was not the fastest coach in the fleet, and the road did not provide many safe overtaking opportunities, and there were no places where I could pull over to let the traffic pass. And then I heard The Noise.

There is something unmistakeable about The Noise of someone about to be sick, and it is a noise that elicits a similar response in me. I was for some time with the ambulance service, and the sight, sound and smell of someone throwing up would usually cause me to honk in sympathy. The same is true of a lot of people, and indeed there is a theory that this is a primal response, from when we used to live in large social groups, in caves, and eat the same food. If one person was sick it was likely to be due to food poisoning and as everyone would have eaten from the communal 'pot' then the group vomit was a survival technique. Knowing this, however, did not make it any better.

The Noise became louder and louder, and was combined with the supervisor's desperate attempts to get him facing somewhere other than her lap. I am here to say that she succeeded and a veritable fountain of pop, chocolate, crisps, medication and lord knows what hit me, hard, in the back of the neck. I was…unhappy with this. It took a lot of effort to keep the coach on the road. It took considerable effort not to throw up. But it took most of my effort not to be most impolite to the supervisor for being so bloody stupid. And I knew that there was nowhere for me to stop for miles. I am fairly sure that driving the coach, in a miasma of second-hand picnic products, whilst the acidic stomach contents first cooled and then chilled, over my white cotton shirt, and hair, and the back of my ears, was the most miserable hour of my life.

I eventually found a lay-by, which by some miracle had a natural stream running out of the rock, and I was able to wash the worst of the explosion out of my hair and ears. Whilst I was doing this, one of the scout leaders provided me with a tee-shirt, whilst my company shirt went in the nearest bin. At least, I decided, things could not get any worse… We were only an hour from Porlock, and maybe two hours from our destination. I could then decant the little, um, dears, and get back home to a proper bath.

Once I was fairly comfortable, and the scouts had cleaned and disinfected the coach, and the smell had been reduced, we all piled back and set off. I am pleased to report that there were no further incidents, until, that is, we reached Porlock Hill.

Porlock Hill is part of the A39, and runs downhill approximately 400 metres in two miles, in a series of bends. It is not a road to be taken lightly, and has been the site of numerous accidents in the past, a lot of which involved coaches which had lost their brakes and hit the stone walls at the bottom of the descent. The gradient is in some places was steeper than one in four, and on the outside, from our point of view, was a 400 metre cliff face, then the Atlantic.

The passengers were looking out of the windows, admiring the stunning views, as we started the descent. The nose of the Bedford dipped and I selected second gear. The engine revs slowly increased as the little diesel engine acted as a brake to slow our passage down the hill. I needed to use as much engine braking as possible, as the old bus had fairly basic brakes, and I didn't want to 'cook' them before we reached the bottom. Eventually, however, the engine braking wasn't enough, and I touched the brake pedal to provide additional arrest to our descent. Except instead of the slight *HISS* of air brakes there was a distinct *THUD*, and the pedal failed to move. I pressed again, harder, and again *THUD*, and no movement of the pedal. Oh heck, this was not a good thing! For a few panicked moments I trod harder and harder on the pedal, each time resulting in the same *THUD* and lack of braking action, and all the time the old bus picked up speed, the engine roaring, and the first bend approaching. The younger passengers, for the most part, thought this was wonderful and all part of the adventure. I, on the other hand, was fairly sure I wasn't having any fun at all. I managed, more through blind luck than on any skill on my part, to get the coach round the first bend, and by that time my head had cleared a bit, and I did what I should have done in the first place. I pulled on the handbrake and killed the engine. We slowed, and stopped.

One of the first instructions the passengers had been given was, "You will not eat, nor will you drink, whilst on the coach." Nevertheless, once I had got my breathing back under control, I looked at the foot pedals, and there, directly under the brake pedal, was a glass cola bottle. This had obviously rolled there as we started down the hill and was just the right size to obstruct the brake pedal. I explained what had happened to the supervisor, who was bemused as to why we had stopped, and had not realised there was any problem until I explained to her how close we had come to becoming part of the scenery. She reminded the passengers of their promise not to eat or drink, and after some more time to catch my breath, we started, and this time completed, our descent.

The rest of the journey was pretty much without incident and I returned to base with an empty coach. However, the two incidents, so close together, had coloured my opinion of coach driving, and by the time I'd arrived at the yard I'd pretty much decided that it was no longer what I wanted. I loved driving, but I wanted something that didn't involve passengers. I was no longer comfortable with having so many lives in my hands, nor indeed happy with the not infrequent occasions when a passenger would become violent or abusive. What I wanted, in fact, was a similar job, involving driving long distances, but with passengers who didn't answer back. A nice, easy, safe job. A job where I would never again get hurt. What could that job be?

Taking the P***

To some people the whole idea of driving trucks on the continent is anathema. To be away from home for extended periods, to be isolated from people who have the same culture and speak the same language can be daunting, but to be honest you can get the same effect driving from Sussex to Sunderland!

For others the idea of being a Continental trucker is what they have aimed for all their lives, and to yet others, like myself, they dread the idea, and yet when they try it they grow to love it.

Continental trucking is not, on most occasions, a structured job. You live from day to day, not knowing where you are going to go to reload, or when. You could spend weeks abroad, loading in one country, delivering in another, reloading in a third, or you could find yourself back in the UK for weeks, doing only local work. You could be flitting around the continent, carrying for different companies, or spending months, or even years on the same contract, carrying the same goods to the same destination. First, however, you actually have to gain employment...

One of the problems faced by a newly qualified HGV driver is that to get a job you need experience, and to get experience you need a job. Unless you are extremely lucky no good company is going to hire a newly qualified driver, which is why a lot of new drivers find themselves working for 'cowboys'. Cowboys are that group of employers who believe that they are above the law and require their workforce to behave illegally purely for profit. I was no exception. I ended up working for a gentleman who will be referred to from now on as Mr Boss.

I'd worked for the company for maybe 3 months and had made it very clear that I would go anywhere, in any vehicle, and with any load, so long as I was home every night. Although I was single, I wanted to be with my parents, siblings and pets, and if I were dating, my Girlfriend du jour. Of course, I ran illegally. Mr Boss did not hold with the concept of drivers needling sleep, nor complying with tachograph rules, and weight regulations were written for people who were not him. However, he knew I wanted to be home at night, with my family and for the most part he endeavoured to make sure that I was. There were the odd occasions when I would be stuck with a night out, but most frequently he would give me warning of these, and if possible my Girlfriend du jour would come with me.

Eventually, one morning he rang me and asked if I had a passport. I informed him in the negative, that it had expired. He told me I'd better get one in a hurry, as I would be shipping out that night to Germany. I told him in no uncertain terms that this was not going to happen and he pointed out that there was any number of drivers who could do my job just as well. I buckled under the threat and got a 1-year visitor's passport from the local post office.

The job, according to Mr Boss, was a sure-fire money-spinner. We'd load at the Ford factory in Halewood and ship to any Ford plant in Germany or Belgium. The catch was that the delivery had to be made within 24 hours of leaving Halewood. This was an ideal job for two drivers, but unfortunately Mr Boss thought that two drivers were better deployed in two trucks, so we did the whole job ourselves.

I was distinctly unhappy with the idea of going abroad. However, I needed the job, so I went.

One of the other contractors doing the job was Paul Ashwell, the gentleman who found himself embroiled in the 'Supergun' affair [1] and imprisoned in Greece. He and I often

---

[1]   In the early 1990s, Matrix Churchill, a Coventry firm, exported some tubes to Iraq. The tubes turned out to be the barrel of a 'supergun.' The person contracted to deliver

found ourselves on the run together. He was easy to recognise, as his Leyland truck had a silhouette of a cannon on each door.

On the occasion in question he and I were parked at the Ford factory in Saarlois in Germany, waiting to get unloaded, when a bright red UK registered truck pulled in to the truck park. It parked up, and the driver leapt out of the cab, and ran over to me. I swear he would have hugged us if I hadn't retreated.

After he stopped flapping, he told me that this was his first trip abroad and he had been slightly lost, for three days in Brussels, ending up in a narrow dead-end street that had required the police to close off several roads whilst he reversed out. To say he was upset would be an understatement. He pleaded with me to allow him to run back with us, and being kind hearted, I acquiesced.

At that time German customs were very concerned about the quantities of diesel that trucks were entering the country with. The maximum you were allowed was 200 litres, and they checked every wagon. I had been told that the easiest way to circumvent the problem and indeed the fines the German officials imposed for every litre over the 200 litre allowance,

---

the load was Paul Ashwell. He was arrested and imprisoned in Greece, and there was considerable effort made to have him freed. The scandal that followed was widely publicised, and brought about the collapse of the Coventry firm, the arrest of its Directors, and considerable dissembling from the Government at the time, as investigation produced evidence of Government sanctioned spying, and a cover-up operation.

Paul made an effort to get his life and business back on track, which was where he was when I met him. Where he is now I have no idea, but I hope that he reads this and remembers me, and I wish him well in the future.

was to try and arrive at the border with the tank nearly empty. It should then be possible to refuel at the services in Luxembourg on the way back and also get a meal and a cup of coffee.

We pulled in to the rather crowded truck park and all went for a meal. The new lad eschewed coffee for a couple of pints, which surprised me, given that he had told us he hadn't eaten for two days. After the meal and drinks we sat and chatted away our 45-minute break, and he told me of the trials and tribulations of his first and, according to him, last trip abroad.

"At least now I'm with you nothing more can go wrong!" he avowed. It has been my experience in life that making claims like that is a bad idea, and so it proved...

We returned to the trucks and he let out a howl of anguish. I looked, and there was a stream of liquid running from under his truck.

"I don't believe it! The radiator must be leaking!" he said, and before I could stop him he had crouched, dipped his finger in the trickle of liquid, and tasted it. As he did so I looked along the side of his truck. There was a large gentleman urinating against the front wheel of his truck, and the stream of urine tricked inexorably under the front of my poor unlucky colleague's truck....When he realised what he had just done, the poor man broke down and cried.

We did, eventually, get him back to Calais and the ferry back to the UK. When we parked up to sort out the customs paperwork he got down on his knees, kissed the ground, and swore that he would never ever go abroad again. As he spoke I had an epiphany. Clearly he was wrong. I realised that I had loved the job. I wanted, no, craved to do it again. After all, it was so easy! I took to driving on the 'wrong' side of the road like a duck to water, and after all, that was all there was to this continental lark. What on earth could ever go wrong?

Roadside Repairs

Life can be full of surprises. I am endlessly amazed at the potential for humour in the most unlikely of places. It is not impossible that my stint in the ambulance service has furnished me with a somewhat skewed sense of humour, but I delight in observing the absurd, the amusing, the wonderfully unlikely. Even the act of driving down a road can be a source of amusement. For me, if maybe not for the unwilling participants...

Having come home from Belgium I had delivered a load in Birmingham and was on my way back home, when I found myself in a small queue of traffic on the M1, heading south. Just up ahead I could see there had been a road traffic accident and a car and a people-carrier were limping off the highway. I pulled in to the hard shoulder, as, having been a member of the emergency services, I felt duty bound to render assistance if possible.

It quickly became clear that I was not, in fact, the first medical practitioner on site. Parked in front of me was a pastel blue Morris Minor. Synapses unused since I left the ambulance service started to twang. Nerves that had relaxed began jangling, the hair on the back of my neck stood up. I knew, I just knew who I was going to face.

Nevertheless, true professional that I was, I grabbed my first aid kit, and got out of the cab. And there she was. Stately as a galleon, scary as a scary thing. The District Nurse. My knees went weak and my skin tried to get back in the truck, but I pressed on, certain that she couldn't be as bad as...

"What do you whant, yhoung mhan?!"

Damn it, knees. Keep me upright. She holds no sway over you any more. Her powers are weak!

"Ay said! What do you WHANT! yhoung mhan?" the Voice demanded, once more. I knew I had to answer. The lore foretold that if a District Nurse asked of you the same question thrice, then your soul was hers, forever.

"Um…please, I'm ex ambulance service, Nurse," I replied, and blow me if I didn't nearly put my hand up in the air before I answered.

She looked me up and down. I probably didn't present a particularly stirring sight. Although later in my driving career I developed the habit of wearing a white shirt, tie and pressed trousers, at this moment I was clad in denim shorts, a teeshirt with a very unfunny joke, and wood and cow-hide clogs.

"Ai dhont think you will be necessaryah. Ai have telephoned the real ambulance people. They will be along shortleah," she said, dismissively, and got back in her blue Minor and drove out into the oncoming traffic, without looking, indicating or making any effort to avoid any oncoming vehicles. When you are a District Nurse, you leave all the organising to the rest of the planet, which obviously will arrange things for your convenience…a few hundred years ago she would have been classed as a witch…

Curious as to what had happened, I wandered further up to the scene of the accident, as my eyes started to water, my sides to shake and I had trouble breathing. Basic first aid requires that when you are faced with an open wound or a bleed site, you apply a sterile dressing. The handbooks suggest newly laundered sheets, clean handkerchiefs or any fresh linen. The problem is, very few people are fortunate enough to actually come across an accident whilst carrying any of the above. The advice continues that you should make do with whatever you have to hand. And she had.

As the local ambulance pulled in behind me, I grasped at the Armco, and lowered myself to the floor, eyes streaming, shoulders shaking with suppressed laughter. In front of me were the four 'victims' of the accident, all men.

It was bad enough that one had a split lip, one had a cut over his eye and one had glass cuts to his cheek. The District Nurse had applied what sterile dressings she had to hand, and so all three were pressing NHS sanitary towels to their faces.

But oh, how sorry I felt for the young lad that had the nose bleed. I won't tell you what dressing she had applied, but the poor sod was stood there, red of face, with a small white piece of string hanging from each nostril…

Something offal this way comes

I suppose that it is only fair, having pointed out how events that happen to other people can provide me with so much delight, to chronicle the (not all that) odd occasion when Murphy steps in to make me the butt of the joke.

People have varied images of truck drivers. To some the song 'I like Trucking' as shown on 'Not the Nine O'Clock News' epitomises the group. Overweight, dim as a penny candle, and endlessly scoffing Yorkie bars as they try to scare little old ladies out of their wits with their air horns.

Others see them as Knights of the Road, ever willing to offer help to stranded fellow drivers, to provide directions to the most obscure of places, and transport as well, if the need arises. To yet others the image is that of windswept and interesting modern day gypsy, endlessly driving their rigs to an unreachable yet beckoning destiny.

Each perception is right, in its own way, and each is entirely wrong. Especially the one suggesting the romance of the job…

"I want you to do me a favour."

These words, taken at face value, are harmless. However, when Mr Boss spoke them they had an undercurrent of meaning. The words themselves were not important. The message was carried by the unspoken word. And the unspoken word said, "I have a particularly nasty job for you. A job I wouldn't do if you were paying me three times the pittance I pay you. A job I have offered to all the other drivers, and which they have laughingly told me to shove where the sun doesn't shine!"

Unfortunately I had been working for Mr Boss for less than a year, and was unaware of his duplicity, and helpfully enquired what the job entailed. Apparently he had a contract with a slaughterhouse to remove pallets of frozen offal to a disposal site. Oh, and the job started at 8pm, which would be nice, as it was the middle of a very hot summer. This, as it happens, would be an important factor in why the job went very wrong very quickly…

7:30 pm saw me at the yard, where I was met by Mr Boss. He looked a little concerned at my attire, but I had dressed for the weather in shorts, sandals and tee shirt. It would, in hindsight, have been nice of him to tell me what he actually knew of the job, but he was worried that if he told me the truth I'd turn around and go home, leaving him to do it. So he remained unhelpfully silent. I took the tractor unit and left the yard, heading for the meat processing plant a mile or so up the road.

On arrival the site foreman took a look at the paperwork.

"Ah, you want trailer 1776, it is parked over there," he said, pointing to a long parking bay full of trailers. I walked over to the row and started looking. I reached the other end, turned round, and walked back. Nope, I couldn't see it, so I went back to the site office, and explained that I couldn't find fridge trailer 1776 in the row at all.

"Fridge trailer? It isn't a fridge, my friend. You're looking for a tipper trailer. Should be easy to find too, as it has been stood in the sun all week, full of offal!"

Ten seconds later I was on the phone to Mr Boss, who denied ever telling me that pallets or fridges were involved. He was so convincing that I started to believe him and question my own sanity. As it turned out, I was later to discover that the guy was more closely related to the weasel than the ape, but that is for later stories…

I found the trailer, using nothing more than my sense of smell. Dear gods, it reeked! I looked for the sheeting to cover it, but one of the company drivers who were doing the same run told me that they didn't sheet the load, as the sheets were then unusable for anything else. When I asked him what they did for load security I was told, "Brake very gently, and deny everything."

My lord, how the trailer stank. I reversed under the coupling, checked the trailer was fastened and climbed on to the back of the truck to fasten the airlines. Whilst there I was able to see into the tipper body. You don't want to know. Really you don't. Okay, but don't say I didn't warn you…

Anything that was not useable by the butchers (which, to be honest, at a time before the ban on mechanically reclaimed meat and spine/brain material wasn't a lot) was in that trailer. And you have to understand that if the butchers wouldn't use it even for pet food, it was not just offal, it was awful. Worse, it had stood, uncovered, in the heat of the summer sun for a week, where flies and other insects could get at it. It roiled. It rolled. It heaved. It fulminated. Things crawled in it. Bubbles rose to the surface and *POPPED* in an oily sludge, producing yet more smell.

See, I told you that you didn't want to know…

8pm, and off we set. Three trucks, each with its cargo of doom. Each driver firm of chin, clear of eye and wobbly of stomach. Two of the three drivers clad in waxed boiler suits and waders. What exactly did they know that I didn't?

We hit the M25, and headed for the Dartford Tunnel, which, before the opening of the bridge, was guaranteed to be busy. The two drivers in the ERFs of the company fleet had pulled some distance ahead of me, as my truck was old, slow and poorly maintained, so when I got to the toll booths I was greeted by a worrying sight. A fleet of Landrovers in Dartford River Crossing logos, surrounding the two trucks. Another Landrover drove over to me, stuck on its blue lights and a 'Follow Me' logo, and escorted me to the hard shoulder.

It turned out that we were persona non grata at the site. They would very much like us to go away. To leave. They would be massively grateful if we would consider turning round and discovering a new route avoiding the M25 tunnel, if we would be so kind. Sadly they were couching all this in words that would cause a nun to blush. They really were not keen on us being there. Stupidly, paying no attention to the warning glances of the other two drivers, I enquired why they were so hostile.

It turned out that on the last expedition from the processing plant to the disposal site, one of the drivers had been less careful with the air brakes on the approach to the tollbooths than was sensible. You may recall I mentioned the lack of sheeting on the trailers? It seems that the sudden application of brakes had caused what we would call 'a load shift' and what the toll road officers referred to as, "throwing ten tonnes of shit at the tollbooths." Apparently there was a scattergun effect when the load left the trailer and quite a number of people got a share of the effluvium.

One girl ended up with a sheep skull pretty much in her lap. Whilst lacking skin or flesh it still had the eyes attached, and they gazed mournfully at her. Apparently flayed sheep skulls are not as cute as the ones still attached to the sheep, and she was now off work and on tranquilisers. The toll collector in another of the booths was so affected by the smell as to projectile vomit over a car, whilst the fumes caused the abandonment of a number of booths, and cars, for a number of days. To be fair, the chaps did have good reason not to want us going through the tunnel...

So, we were unceremoniously turned round, and sent away. The officials didn't care where we went, just that we went. So, we turned round, and went all the way back along the M25, anti-clockwise, which is not, on the whole, the most sensible way of getting to Canterbury from the north of the country.

One of the things you see on motorways and especially the M25 in summer is convertible cars with the tops down, tailgating lorries. Not so that night, strangely. Any car that drew up behind us very quickly pulled way back or passed very rapidly.

At about 1am we pulled off the motorway, and drove down quiet country lanes, and eventually up a narrow winding track. It only qualified for the name road rather than cycle path because nobody in their right mind would want to ride a bike down it. The smell of corruption was overwhelming. Good lords, and I had thought the trailer smelt bad!

We turned into a yard, lit with powerful yellow floodlights. My command of the English language is not sufficient to describe what confronted me. I will try, but however bad it may sound, believe me when I say it was in actuality ten times worse.

At one end of the yard was an old brick building. Windowless, but with a multitude of vents, it steamed in the demonic light. Had Dante witnessed this place his Ninth Level of Hell would not have been ice, and Judas would have had much more to concern him than chilblains. (Incidentally, did you know that Judas was a red-head? That's right. Judas is carrot).

In a hut adjacent to the building were three men in orange boiler suits. One acknowledged us with a wave and then wandered out. He was an imposing being, having shoulder length grey hair and a massive beard. We stopped the wagons and got out. The two other drivers started pulling on long rubber boots. What did they know that I didn't?

After a brief chat, the two drivers wandered over, and told me that we had to tip the load in the courtyard. I looked, and it was at this point I decided that when I got back home Mr Boss was going to die. The 'courtyard' was in fact an area of about an acre, possibly of concrete, but mainly of offal, several feet deep. I watched as the first driver reversed his wagon in to the slurry, and got out of the cab. And I realised the significance of the boots.

The tipper trailers had a small diesel engine to power the tipping hydraulics and it was mounted half way down the chassis. It was started by a crank handle, and this meant that you had to wade through the gunk to reach it. I looked down at my spindly white legs and sandals. Oh…goody…

I will draw a veil over the next twenty minutes, except to say that there are nights when I wake in the early hours, screaming.

Having pulled the wagon clear I availed myself of the hosepipe on the side of the building. It was meant to be used for washing the wheels of the trucks before we left. I had a far better use for it. Whilst I was washing myself down I observed the chap with the beard shovelling some of the goop down a ramp into the processing plant. And then pick up a sandwich and start eating it. ***SHUDDER.***

In my time I have seen, heard and smelt a lot of things that would curdle the stomach of less hardy folk, and not even flinched. However, I have to say that it took me several weeks before I could look a bowl of beef broth in the eye again without breaking into a sweat. And it took me several more weeks before I managed to get the smell out of the truck...

Customs Curiosity

One of the more, um… interesting aspects of the driving job was that it forced you into close contact with that curious mindset, 'The Official.'

Given to wearing impressive uniforms, often with even more impressive hats, these individuals have a job to do, and they are not going to let petty annoyances such as common sense and humanity get in their way.

That really isn't a fair statement. For every 'Official' you meet you are likely to encounter tens of 'officials' who do their job so well and so unobtrusively that you never notice them. To these people I offer my humble apology, for the book will contain quite a few references to 'Officials' whilst barely acknowledging the existence of the 'official' who has made my job, my day, and my life just that little bit easier. To those people, those unacknowledged heroes of every day life, I salute you.

To the 'Official' however…

The job of carrying Ford car parts to Germany and Belgium was, for the most part, uneventful. Once we had been given suitable wagons we just got on with the work and tried, to the best of our abilities, to make our runs legal. It was not fun having to try and tiptoe a 38 tonne truck past every police car and weighbridge, trying to look inconspicuous. However, The Boss had decided that he didn't have to bother with HGV road tax when ordinary car tax would do, so we were regularly getting pulled. It then fell to us to explain that yes, we knew the vehicle was not legally taxed, but that we were not responsible for that, and the very nice police officer would have to speak to our boss. I have no idea how many summonses he got about this, but I should imagine it ran into the high tens, possibly touching a hundred. Yet still he persisted in doing it.

The one bonus of the Ford job was that you almost always came back empty. The job paid well enough that a one way trip was worthwhile. Well, I say it paid well. Certainly Mr Boss made money on it, but we poor drivers were still getting paid £120 per week, whether we worked in the UK or abroad, and whether we went home every night or once a fortnight...

One thing Mr Boss did not mind was his drivers carrying passengers. This meant that I could at least take Girlfriend du jour with me when she was on holiday, so I got to see her. And it was on just one of these occasions when we were honoured by a demonstration of the thoroughness of the Customs Official.

Disembarking from the P&O ferry, we queued at the customs station. Now, frequently we would just be allowed through 'on the nod,' but on this occasion a young Customs Official came out and asked if he could search the truck. I nodded and climbed out of the cab, paperwork in hand.

"What have you got on board?" he asked.

"Glider engines," I grinned.

He looked puzzled and wandered round to the back of the trailer, and asked me to open up.

I got him to check the customs seal on the trailer, then broke it, and opened up the back. He looked in to a totally empty trailer.

"But I thought you said you had glider eng....OH. I get it. Yes, very good."

He did not seem best pleased... He then asked if I would mind him searching the cab of the truck and again I nodded my consent. He climbed up into the cab and started poking around, opening cupboards, looking into carrier bags of dirty laundry...I watched in some amusement as he discovered the bag into which Girlfriend du jour had placed her worn unmentionables...

Finally he sat in the driver's seat and asked if I understood my customs allowance. I agreed that I did indeed.

"Then why is it," he inquired "that you have down here on the form that you have 400 cigarettes. You should know that your personal allowance is only 200"

"Yes, I know. 200 for me and 200 for her," I replied and pointed to my girlfriend in the passenger seat. He looked over, saw her, apparently for the first time, yelped, and fell headlong out of the truck…

That's right. He'd searched the cab, and totally failed to see my young lady in the passenger seat. Which is funny all by itself. But he'd also found her bag of used drawers. What the heck did he think that I would be doing with a bag full of lacy skimpies? No, on second thoughts, keep the answer to yourself, for I do not want to know!

<u>Tragedy</u>

When you drive for a living you will inevitably come across road traffic accidents.
Some are fairly minor. Some not so.

I thought long and hard about including this story. It was the hardest decision I have
had to make. In the end I decided that I had to, as a monument to 'Tracey', and as an
explanation as to why I now consider drink-drivers the very scum of the earth. I confess that
before this incident I did not drink much, but would occasionally go out and have one or two
drinks with the lads. What was the worst that could happen? I was a good driver. A couple of
beers wouldn't make a difference.

This incident changed my mind, and my life. It played a big part in making me the
person I am today. If, when you read it, it makes you think twice about having 'one for the
road' then maybe I would have done someone some good.

Names and locations have been changed. My feelings never can be...

There is a pub in Heysham, on the way to the docks. I don't recall the name; we all
called it the Nuclear Arms, due to its location near to the power station.

On this particular Sunday night I had taken a trailer load of toilet rolls to the docks,
for shipping to Ireland. After dropping it off, I went to our agent's Portakabin to see which
trailer I would be bringing back.

As it happened, on this particular night there was none to collect, so I would be going
home "Bobtail", or unit only, with no trailer. This meant I would be home early. Result.

There were a few cars leaving from the Isle of Man ferry, and I tucked in behind the
queue, waiting to exit the docks. The car in front was a Peugeot estate car, and sat in the rear-

facing occasional seat in the back was a young girl. Her name, I discovered later, was Tracey, and that day was her 12th birthday.

The Peugeot went through, and I stopped at the barriers.

A couple of minutes later, I happened upon a scene of devastation. The Peugeot estate was stopped at the traffic lights. Embedded in the back was a blood red Peugeot 205 GTI.

Panicked, I grabbed my first aid kit from the truck, and rushed over to see what was happening. The driver of the 205 was yelling abuse, so he was okay. I looked in to the mess in the back of the estate car, and for the first time I understood what was meant by 'my heart froze.'

I struggled in through the back window to the poor child.

Tracey was in a lot of pain. The floor and rear door of the car had folded in, crushing her from mid chest down. From the chest up she was cut by the flying glass. She was pale, and not crying, but talking quite calmly about what had happened. I started trying to clean her up, and calm her down.

We talked about the party she had been to in the Isle of Man with her auntie and her cousin. She told me she wanted to be a lorry driver when she grew up, like her uncle Trevor. I told her about my dogs, and she told me about her cats and her pet rat.

The emergency services turned up. They were concerned that I should get out and let one of them in, but I explained that I had spent several years as a paramedic, before I left to drive buses. It was decided that as I had achieved a rapport with her and was physically in there. I would remain, administer the IV and any supporting medication required whilst the fire brigade cut us out.

Over the next thirty five minutes we got to know each other very well. She wasn't too upset when I set up a saline drip, and she accepted my checking her blood pressure and pulse. I was terrified. I had not often seen such low blood pressure in a conscious person.

As the emergency services took her parents from the front of the car, and started cutting away the roof and sides, I got her to smile by telling jokes. She was not, to my surprise, scared by the noises going on around her. She was briefly worried that her mum would be cross when she saw that there was blood on her jumper, but I told her she would be so pleased to see her daughter she wouldn't worry. I promised, if her mum was cross, to buy her another jumper just like it. She decided she'd like one with a sheep on it. No. On second thoughts, she'd like one with a lorry on "just like yours."

Thirty five minutes it took for the fire brigade to make everything safe for extraction. And then Tracey looked at me and said, "It's alright. It doesn't hurt any more." And then did something I have not to this day forgiven her for.

She died.

The fire brigade got me out and the police were around. So was the driver of the 205. Apparently he had come out of the Nuclear Arms drunk and tried to drive home. He was still cursing the driver and family of the estate car for stopping at the red light.

I drove back to the yard, handed in the keys to the truck and asked them to take me off that job, effective immediately. I could no longer envisage going to Heysham. I could no longer pass the spot. I have never been back to Heysham since.

Her parents were badly injured in the crash. Her mother was pregnant at the time with what would turn out to be Tracey's little brother. I stayed in contact with them for a while, but...the pain of the memory was too great. I understand that they moved to Spain to forge a new life for themselves. I'm sure her memory lives on in them as it does in me.

Gas Trick Flue

I had settled into the rut of driving from Halewood to Fords and actually became quite comfortable with it. Were it not for an act of blind stupidity on the part of Mr Boss, combined with an incredible piece of luck, I would possibly be tramping up and down the road from Halewood to the docks to this very day...

Although initially I was reluctant to take the truck abroad I soon actually started to enjoy the work, and in spite of working hours that were long and illegal, for several months I had a lot of fun hauling loads to Germany for Ford. However, there was one thing that I was unaware of, and that my boss had decided to ignore in the hopes that I would sort the problem out for him.

At that time I was pulling the trailers with a Volvo F6 day cab tractor unit. This is not a vehicle designed to be slept in, and for months I'd been working around this by sticking up newspaper round the windows and sleeping across the seats in a sleeping bag. Whilst this was not exactly comfortable it was, at least, possible.

The thing that I was unaware of manifested itself on the 1st October, when I arrived at the German border with Belgium. The police officer on duty came out, looked at the truck, and promptly told me to turn round and go home. It soon became clear to me that Germany operated a rule whereby you could not enter the country after 1st October unless you had a form of cab night heating, as the weather began to deteriorate badly and they quite rightly didn't want idiotic foreign drivers freezing to death and cluttering up their countryside.

A hurried phone call persuaded Mr Boss to send the only tractor unit that we had with a night heater, and he told me he'd make arrangements for my truck to be fitted with one. He sounded quite perky about the idea. This, in itself, should have put my on my guard...

I met the other truck driver and we swapped trailers. This meant that I ended up having to go to Spain and because of Murphy's Law I ended up there for two weeks. No change of clothes, no food, and little money. I have to tell you, that was a long two weeks. It was also the first time I'd been to Spain by truck and I loved it. On returning to the UK, tired, hungry and smelly, Mr Boss showed up with the night heater.

Oh my…it was something the shape of a traditional flying saucer, with a grille at the top and a spout at the side. It came with a clear plastic bottle of liquid. It was, in effect, a paraffin heater! I asked for the instructions and was told not to worry about it. All I had to do, apparently, was fill it with the liquid and light it. No worries, it would turn itself off if it was tipped over. And like a fool, I believed him.

Back again to Germany, and the Police Officer tried to get me to turn around again, but I showed him the heater. He conferred with his book of rules and his colleagues, and grudgingly they allowed me in to the country. I smiled, waved and set out for Saarlois and the Ford factory.

Having unloaded the body panels, and reloaded empty cages, I pulled out of the factory and parked up in the truck park. It was too early for bed, so I wandered into the village, found a bar, had a coffee, and then went for a walk. I happened across a Pizza place and bought a chicken pizza and a bottle of cola, and then returned to the truck.

Pizza consumed, I stuck pages of The Sun to the windows, filled and lit the heater, and then retired to my bed.

The next thing I knew was being in the open, in daylight, with a blinding headache, a massive pain in my chest and an oxygen mask. Ye gods, I hurt! A paramedic was kneeling beside me and one of my co-drivers was beside him. It took a while to find out what had happened. My co-driver and friend Carl had arrived in the early hours of the morning, unloaded and retired to bed. His alarm had gone off at six and he came over to see what time

I would be leaving, but couldn't get an answer. Eventually he'd attracted the attention of a security guard, and they'd smashed the window and gained entry, to find me very unwell across the seats. By very unwell, I mean not breathing, blue, and cold. The ambulance paramedics had to restart my heart.

It took me a week to recover, another week to get home, and several more days to find out what had happened. Mr Boss, it seems, was not happy with buying the heaters and the fuel to go in them, so had simply bought paraffin. As you know, boys and girls, you should never use a paraffin heater in a room without adequate ventilation. This burner had been designed to run on a much safer fuel and it did not react well to paraffin. Subsequent investigation revealed that the fumes it gave off were noxious. I had been very lucky. If Carl had not been diverted to Saarlois, and had not come across to see me, then I would no doubt have died from Carbon Monoxide poisoning. As it was, my chest and heart suffered not inconsiderable after effects and for some years after I had to have regular health checks. As luck would have it there was no real long-term damage done, but it was only through sheer luck that I do not have to dictate this through the medium of a medium.

Mr Boss and I had words when I was fit enough to go back to work. Strangely it did not take me long to persuade him that the trucks we had were not suitable for the work and before long we were the proud owners of two second-hand Iveco trucks, with bigger engines and night heaters. Which, incidentally, didn't work very often, or very well, but at least he'd made an effort. My real continental truck driving life had started!

Dodgy

The idea of driving on the continent can be off-putting to some people. Driving on the wrong side of the road, seeing road-signs in a foreign language, having to remember driving regulations…it can be very disconcerting.

There was only one thing I found difficult, and it was, and is, very specific. If I returned to the UK from Calais to Dover, Eastern Docks, and if I had to head north along Jubilee Way, I was fine until I reached the roundabout at the top of the hill. Then I had to stop, and wait for a car to go round, and then follow it. For some reason I could not remember which way to go round that one, specific roundabout.

Sometimes, of course, it is not me out of step, but the rest of the world…

"Look, it's a dead easy job. All you have to do is take the tractor unit and go and pick up the trailer. It's in Valencia, at the garage where Alan is getting the Volvo fixed."

I was dubious. Mr Boss' 'easy jobs' had a tendency to become ludicrously complex, because he either 'forgot' certain details, 'forgot' to make arrangements that he promised, or downright lied. However, the idea of a tractor-only run to Valencia, then straight back with half a trailer load of cardboard car door trims did seem like the ideal trip for a spring weekend. I agreed. You'd think by then I would have known, wouldn't you?

I was, once again, in the little Volvo F6, the day-cabbed unit that was not intended to be a long distance continental truck. A day-cabbed truck is one in which the cab is designed only to be used during the day. There is no facility for resting or sleeping, whereas a sleeper-cabbed truck has, as the name suggests, a sleeping compartment behind the driving seat. I put up with the wisecracks from the other drivers.

"What are you doing? Road testing for Matchbox?" "What does it want to be when it grows up?", because I knew something they didn't. I knew that I was totally out of my mind to be doing the job with that truck, but loved the job too much to care.

The problems started when I was half way across Spain. At about 2pm, with no warning, there was a massive snowstorm. With no trailer there was no weight on the back axle, and being such an old truck there were no driver aids such as anti-lock brakes or wheel spin reduction. For a couple of hours the driving was quite interesting...

Valencia was under several inches of snow when I finally found Alan. I wandered into the café that abutted the workshop that held his broken Volvo, and greeted him.

"Broke the back axle. That trailer is heavy!"

I was confused. " Heavy? It is supposed to be partly filled with door cards."

"Yeah. But the rest is full of car doors. And engines."

Mr Boss had done it to me again!

Strangely, when I rang him, he wasn't available. His wife told me to contact the company we were contracting for, which I quickly did. When I rang them they made it clear that Mr Boss was fully aware of what the load consisted of and that the trailer had to be back at Poole within three days. Oh...goody!

Alan and I exchanged views on Mr Boss, then he helped me to couple the trailer and I left. Very slowly...

At this time the BP Truckstop in Bordeaux was still under construction and so the favourite stopping place for truck drivers was at St-Genise de Saintonge. We called it 'Saintes.' It is on the National 137, and for trucks heading for Cherbourg it was just one day's drive away.

I pulled in the truck park at 6pm and the snow was falling heavily. I was absolutely shattered. To get there had been a struggle, as my poor little truck was pulling something in the region of ten tonnes more than its design weight.

I stopped the engine and as the snow settled around me, I covered the windscreen with copies of the Sun newspaper, set the alarm for 2:45am, tried to get comfortable over the seats, avoiding the handbrake and fell asleep.

My alarm clock at the time was an 'amusing' device, in the shape of a cockerel and it crowed. My how I laughed when I saw it. How I giggled when I bought it. How I hated it that morning...

Getting out of bed was always a struggle. One's body had to form an S shape to try and avoid the gearstick and the handbrake lever. There was little danger of taking the brake off, but it was three inches long, and no matter where you lay it wanted to become intimate with your buttocks.

No time for coffee. I changed the tachograph disc, checked that my driving break, at least, was legal, fired up the engine and started off. Around me the car park, the trucks and the road were swathed in a blanket of white. To my recently asleep mind it was if the whole place had been draped in a duvet. It was hard to make out where the car park ended and the road began. It was, I discovered fairly quickly, equally hard to see where the road side ended and the grass verge, ditch or pavement began. This was going to be an interesting trip back!

As I crested a small hill I saw headlights approaching me. Two or three cars in line. The front car started flashing its lights at me, rapidly. He was on my side of the road! Or was I on his?

In my still semi-asleep state I considered the possibilities. Either I, a lone English truck driver, had awoken and sleepily driven onto the wrong lane of the carriageway, or several locals had decided to play a joke. At the last minute I swerved onto 'my' side of the road and the convoy of cars went past, horns blaring, fists being waved out of the windows. Each car had a GB registration and a GB sticker. And approaching me was another set of headlights, flashing ,madly. For now I really was on the wrong side of the road.

Having sorted out in my mind exactly where I was supposed to be, I pressed on again, as the snow continued falling. All was well, until I approached La Rochelle and in front of me was a long queue of cars. I eased in behind the last and realised that they had been there for some considerable time, as the snow was thick on them. I got out of the truck and spoke to the gentleman in the rearmost car. He explained that the slipway that he, and I, needed to get from La Rochelle to Cherbourg was closed, due to snow. Workmen were clearing it, but they had been there for over an hour and expected to be there for at least two more.

I thanked the gentleman and returned to my truck, turned off the engine, and settled down to wait…

How remarkably peaceful it was! All external noise seemed to be damped by the snow. One or two of the cars ran their engines to keep warm, but the most prominent noise was the susurration of the snowflakes, drifting, falling, hypnotic in the light of the yellow streetlamps.

My hands caressed the satin-smooth skin of her shoulders, my fingertips stroking her throat as they slid down the gentle curve of her bosom to her full, magnificent breasts. As I cupped the left breast it went Dee!....intrigued, I caressed the right. Dah!...I had quite a rhythm going when I suddenly realised it was a police siren, and woke up...

Startled, I looked for the source of the noise. On the other carriageway a Peugeot, resplendent in its blue livery, red, amber and blue lights on the top piercing the snow-laden gloom, the word 'Gendarme' in white on its flanks. What was upsetting them?

I looked in my mirrors to see who they were waving at. Behind me a long line of cars, trucks and busses was becoming visible as the daylight started to break through the stygian darkness. I could see nothing behind me to warrant such excited behaviour, so I looked to see if it was any of the cars in…front?

There were no cars in front!

Oops.

It would seem that I had fallen asleep, lulled by the peace and quiet and in doing so had become an unintentional traffic jam.

Oh, and I managed to catch the boat, by about five minutes…

The Pain in Spain

It is possible that I may be misrepresenting the job of Continental Truck driver somewhat. For every yin there is a yang. For every up, a down. For every easy job a…let me explain…

My very first trip to Spain made me fall hopelessly in love with the place and the people. Sadly it is something like twenty years since I last visited, apart from a wonderful week when two dear friends of mine invited me to partake of an off-roading holiday in Andorra. Even that short return visit rekindled my love of the place. Even if Spain has tried to kill me on at least three occasions…

The first occasion was whilst I was delivering Blackpool illuminations to The Castle in Barcelona. I was, for reasons I have never managed to discover, delivering to The Castle the following:-

One Large Plastic Illuminated Postman Pat.

One Large Plastic Illuminated Postal Van.

One Large Plastic Illuminated Cat.

Two hundred and fifty Wuzzle's bottoms.

I had no idea at the time what a Wuzzle was, but have since found out that they are combination animals. For example one is called Bumblion, a combination of lion and bumble-bee. Of course, they are characters from children's TV and therefore only the better characteristics of each animal are manifested in each of the mythical beasts.

Excuse me? What are the better characteristics of a bee and a lion? Does this beast have the capacity to sting you to death before it eats you, but chooses not to do so out of the kindness of its feline heart? And Eleroo. A cross between a kangaroo and an elephant! I'm still trying to imagine what would be the effect of an animal the size of an African Elephant hopping across your back garden. I'm guessing you'd need a JCB to discover whether your garden gnomes survived the attack. But I digress…

The whole concept was so bizarre that whilst the team were unloading the trailer, I went across the road and took pictures. As it happened there was an old wreck of a Renault 4 abandoned at the kerbside outside the main entrance, so I used it as a makeshift tripod whilst taking pictures of the load coming off and being carried past what turned out to be inflatable illuminated sarcophagi. It was obvious that the team that were unloading the trailer were quite skilled and before long they had completed the job. The trailer was empty and I was ready to return to the TIR park, to see my agent, and sort out a reload.

I am not the most striking of individuals. I don't have 'presence.' People don't stop what they are doing and stare when I walk into a room. I actually enjoy being inconspicuous. So you can imagine my surprise when I wandered into the office of my agent and the assistant shrieked, dropped her coffee and fled the room!

Moments later my agent came out of his office and beckoned me, whilst gabbling on that he thought I was dead. Bemused, I followed him into his office, wherein he had a little black-and-white TV, whilst reassuring him that I had not, to my knowledge, shuffled off these mortal coils. He pointed to the TV, which was showing a local news program. I watched for a few moments and then, as my fairly limited Spanish began to understand what the rapidly speaking reporter was saying, my stomach turned over.

Apparently, a bomb of several hundred pounds of explosives had detonated outside The Castle causing mayhem, death and destruction. A lorry driver had been badly injured, police and soldiers had died in the blast. The bomb, it turned out, had been packed in the shell of a Renault 4 at the front of the castle. The same Renault 4 that I had used, not 90 minutes earlier, as a tripod.

As the news story unwound, we worked out that the explosion had happened no more than twenty minutes after I had had my paperwork signed. Had the crew who unloaded the trailer been less efficient, or I had been a little later with the delivery, then I could have been resting against the Renault when it exploded…

The second occasion was at a place called Vic, just outside Barcelona. I was in the process of delivering chopped polythene pieces to a factory near the fire station and had stopped on a hill just outside the town, so I could have some lunch.

As I sat drinking a cold cola, I watched another Renault 4 drive past, heading down the hill into town. About three seconds later my brain caught up with my eyes and ears. There was no driver in the car and the engine wasn't running. I looked down the hill to see what was going on, and my heart lurched.

At the bottom of the hill was a police centre, with police office, a courtyard and housing. The car had gone through the courtyard and the explosives had detonated. Later I was to find out that many of the dead and injured were women and children playing in the courtyard. I understand the politics, but I don't care about them. No organisation can claim any moral high ground when it bases its protests on the slaughter of the innocents. No matter what ETA may claim, it can never take the moral high ground, and any political statements, any deals, any progress it makes toward gaining Basque independence will be forever tainted by the souls of their victims.

The third occasion required the combined efforts of the Guarda Civil, twenty tonnes of paper, the cack-handed mechanical ineptitude of Mr Boss and a paella, and can be read elsewhere in the book, under the title 'Paper paper everywhere.'

Oh I do like to be beside the seaside!

Although the life of a driver can be lonely, Mr Boss was happy for me to carry passengers. Often this would be Girlfriend du jour. But just occasionally...

My first trip to Portugal was supposed to be a quick in and out in between my usual tramping work all over Europe. I had a load of girders to deliver just north of Porto and a load to collect from Jerez in Spain once I was tipped. The trip was scheduled so I arrived on the Friday, got tipped Saturday morning having cleared customs in Porto, then straight out into Spain again, ready to load on Monday morning. It was mid July, the sun was shining, and everything was all right with the world.

As I pulled up to the Spanish/Portuguese border at Villar Formoso I was met with a long line of trucks queuing to go through. I pulled in to the end of the line and parked, then got out to see what was causing the hold-up. The third truck I came to was a British registered wagon and so I asked the driver if he knew what the problem was.

"From what I gather there's either a strike or a holiday. I can't make it out."

The pair of us walked further down the line and I asked the driver of a French truck what was causing our unscheduled stop. He shrugged in the typical Gallic way. He too was baffled and he accompanied us as we strolled up the line. A Spanish registered truck had its driver's door open and the driver was sat inside reading a newspaper, so in my newly learned Spanish I enquired after the health of his toothbrush. He looked at me askance. I did a quick mental shuffling of Spanish nouns and managed to establish that the reason for the hold-up was preparations for a bank holiday on Monday of which none of us were aware. I passed the information on to my French friend, who, it transpired, spoke Spanish rather better than I did, and my English compatriot, who was impressed with my linguistic prowess, and I was not going to tell him any different!

Very slowly the queue abated and eventually I was waved through the rather primitive shed area of the Portuguese customs area, and into the country. There I sampled, for the first time, the Portuguese road system. When The Gods made Portugal they wanted to make it really big, but discovered that when it was shown on a map it made Spain look silly and so they hammered the edges until it fit better, and as a result the landmass got all wrinkled and crinkly. Now, it is possible that you may remember your geography teacher talking about tectonic plates, continental drift and other such guff. Personally I prefer my version. Either way, the route from the border to Porto was along some of the twistiest and steepest roads I have ever encountered.

As I crawled my way up an incline some miles into the country my eyes fell upon a vision, an apparition, a…what the hell was it? Walking along the road was somebody apparently clad in nineteen fifties drawing room curtains, with an Afghan Hound around its neck. As I drew nearer the Afghan Hound resolved into a very furry collar on a Parka, whilst the nineteen fifties drawing room curtains resolved into…nineteen fifties drawing room curtains. Purple paisley pattern fabric, red sashes, velvet, silks, cotton, all amalgamated into something that may have been trousers, may have been a skirt, but was, without a doubt, English. And the whole person was hitch-hiking. Intrigued, I stopped to see if it wanted a lift.

It turned out to be a very attractive young lady. Gratefully she climbed into the truck and threw her rucksack into the back.

"Hi! I'm Echo."

"Who?"

"Echo!" she grinned at me.

I asked her what she was doing and she told me that she was going round Europe on a pound a day. Clearly I looked askance. She explained that she had finished University and was having a gap year before deciding whether to continue education or look for work. In the meantime she had allotted three hundred pounds and set out to hitchhike and walk around Europe, spending as little money as possible and depending on the kindness of strangers. I looked at her again. Tall, slender, waist length brown hair, startling blue eyes set in a perfect face. I was smitten. It occurred to me that if she had the same effect on other European males as she had on me she would probably return home with most of the three hundred unspent.

I asked where she wanted taking and she said that wherever I was going would be good for her. She was in no hurry and when I told her I was going to Porto she was quite happy to accompany me. I was happy to let her. And so we set off.

Anyone who knows me will tell you that I am shy around strangers and more so around the opposite sex. Echo, however, was easy to talk to and even easier to listen to. As we toiled along the road between the boarder and the motorway, we discussed everything and nothing, we **OOOHED** and **AAAHED** at the scenery and within an hour it was as if we had known each other for years. Truth to tell, I can't remember much about the journey to the coast, but before long we had reached the motorway that runs between Porto and Lisbon, and shortly after that we arrived in Porto.

Following the signs to the TIR yard I was concerned that there was little HGV traffic on the road. However, my concern became alarm when we arrived at the TIR park to find that apart from one Spanish registered truck it was totally empty. I pulled to a halt and we got out to see if we could make any sense out of what was happening. I was not a little impressed when Echo asked, in Spanish, what was occurring and nodded and chatted for a while. She then turned to me and explained that a bank holiday had been declared and no work would be done today, over the weekend or Monday. As a result, any chance I had for a reload was blown out of the water. I would have to park up, clear Customs on Tuesday and get tipped, and then hope to get a reload a soon as was possible. The Spaniard suggested that British truckers usually congregated at The Atlantica Bar and pointed out on a map where it was located. He assured me that there was plenty of room to park and I should take the trailer as well, for security. Echo seemed quite delighted at the idea of stopping for the weekend and I was not going to argue with her, so we set out for Matosinhos and The Atlantica Bar.

The bar turned out to be a large single story building, literally on the beach and beside it were maybe half a dozen British and Dutch trucks, parked on compacted sand, right there on the beach. Oh my! Mid summer, Portugal, with three days off, parked on the beach, next to a bar, with a beautiful girl as company. What could be better?

Well, what could be better became better later that evening, when I suggested that Echo might like to borrow my sleeping bag and sleep in the trailer. She looked at me and at the back bunk.

"What is wrong with me sleeping there?" she enquired.

"Well that's where I sl....Ooooh! Nothing. Nothing at all"

It was a more innocent time. STDs were the numbers you put in front of a telephone number if you were calling from out of town. Aids were a slimming supplement. We were not fettered by mores and vows of chastity. We were not bound by promise of celibacy and faithfulness. In truth, the only thing that bound and fettered us was gravity and the small area that was an HGV bunk bed. Good taste requires that I draw a veil over the more physical aspects of that night, but I trust you will allow me a brief moment to remember and marvel that I didn't dislocate anything major.

We leaned a lot more about each other that night. I leaned that oral sex did not involve talking at all and she learned that the distance between the bottom bunk and the top bunk was exactly five inches below where your head reaches when you sit up suddenly. I learned that she was incredibly sensitive when touched in a certain way and she learned that the distance between the bottom bunk and the top bunk was exactly five inches below where your head reaches when you sit up suddenly. I learned that her command of basic Anglo-Saxon was even more impressive than her command of Spanish and she learned that I knew how a gentleman apologises to a lady he has wronged. I learned that more than once a night was possible, when you were motivated strongly enough and she learned that more than four times a night was not possible without the aid of trained medical professionals. I learned that she was warm and cuddly and she learned that I snored. I learned that she intended to stay with me for a little while longer, at least, and she learned that I giggled. And people say that learning is boring…

The next morning, when I awoke, she was gone. Briefly I was mortified, but I realised that I should not really have expected anything else. I was an ordinary truck driver, of little or no merit, and she was an incredibly attractive, intelligent young lady. To her I must have seemed a toy, a means of transport a…there was a note on the dashboard.

"Hi, I've gone for a swim. Get breakfast cooking for when I get back."

I have never really understood why, but I find a woman in a swimsuit at least as sexy as a woman out of one. Possibly the seduction of the concealed. Possibly the promise, the lure of what is to come. Possibly I am just weird. In any case, when she returned, in a shining pink and blue swimsuit I nearly burned my sausage.

Later that day we met up with some of the other drivers and went to the Atlantica Bar for a meal. On the menu was homemade vegetable soup and as I adore soups, I ordered a bowl. Marco, the waiter, came out with the order. Marco, the waiter, had a problem. Marco, the waiter, was stoned. As he came over, he tripped or stumbled, and the hot soup tipped neatly into my lap. Fortunately the sea was a few seconds away, at a dead run, and it provided a cooling solution. Eventually I emerged from the ocean, and trudged back to the truck, changed into dry clothing, then returned to the bar. The owner was stood at the door, and angrily waved a bill in my face. She wanted to charge me for the soup! Echo wandered up and explained what had happened, and I offered to show her the damage. The owner relented and offered me free food and drink for the remainder of my stay. I never did get around to trying the soup, however.

Sunday saw me up and cooking breakfast as Echo again went swimming, and shortly after that we both set out to walk into Porto and partake of some sightseeing. Regimented rows of white walled, red tiled buildings rose from the sea up into the hills. Designed for keeping port stored in exactly the right condition to mature; now they were beginning to be redeveloped into what was, at that time, a burgeoning tourist industry. As European money had been poured into its neighbour, Spain, now it was beginning to be routed into Portugal, but at the time of my visit Portugal was still an incredibly poor country. The jarring dissonance of wealth and paucity, affluence and effluent, was plain to see. An area of white stone villas segued uncomfortably into a shantytown of tin and breezeblock, then into an industrial sprawl of soot-belching chimneys, steel refineries, smoke and flame. It was simultaneously awesome and depressing beyond measure. We were entranced.

All of a sudden the smell of smoke assaulted our senses and in front of us a wooden building lit like a brazier. A few people left the building, at some speed, and it became apparent that it was a building used, not surprisingly, for the production of port. The fire drill was carried out with sufficient precision to make me think that this was not an uncommon occurrence and everybody appeared accounted for, so, always willing to watch a free show, I sat on the grass bank and observed.

Now, having seen the apparent haphazard nature of the rest of the Portuguese infrastructure I was looking forward to seeing how the fire brigade performed. However, I was really not expecting the arrival of a white Fiat 500 car, which stopped outside the burning property and disgorged four burly guys in black uniforms. One of them ran to the front of the car and opened the boot, the Fiat being rear-engined, and extracted a length of hose, then whilst the other three grabbed at the nozzle-end of the fire hose he ran with the reel to the fire hydrant. Unfortunately for him, but to our utter delight, he had failed to notice something that Echo and I realised fairly quickly. About a hundred yards from the fire hydrant the hose ran out, became taut, and his progress came to a sudden halt and both he and his three colleagues ended up on the floor. After regaining their composure a huddle occurred, a consensus reached and the hose was reeled, deposited back in the boot, and the four returned to the car and drove away. We sat for a while longer, but as the building burned and the recent occupants stood about smoking, watching and chatting, nobody else turned up, and eventually, as the building fell in on itself we left and headed back to the truck, the Atlantica Bar, the ocean and another night together.

Nervous Breakdown

Breakdowns were a regular occurrence whilst working for Mr. Boss. Occasionally the truck broke down. Often the driver broke down. Frequently both broke down. When we were in the UK this was a problem, as he had no breakdown cover whatsoever, but when the truck broke down abroad it was a nightmare...

Tuesday morning dawned bright and sunny. Echo was rather less sunny. The few days of rest and relaxation had made her (and, to be honest, me) used to rising at the crack of 10am, having a leisurely swim and a breakfast. 6am was unforgivably early, but work took precedence over bodily comfort and so whilst Echo dressed I checked the trailer over, did the daily truck checks, put in a new tachograph disk, and checked the map. We set off to the TIR park, where we rapidly received customs clearance, and were given a delivery address of a building site just north of Porto. I checked the map, and off we went.

Whilst the main transport infrastructure of Portugal was being improved by stages, the less tourist-oriented routes were rather less well maintained, and the road I found myself on was an amalgam of tarmac, gravel, granite and chalk. In some places the demarcation of road and verge was indicated not by a change of structure, but by little orange and red painted wooden posts. Other areas could only be dignified by the name "road" by the fact vehicles were using them to drive along. Be that as it may, we made good progress and Echo and I were chatting inconsequentialities and admiring the views, when I noticed that vehicles travelling in the other direction were flashing their lights at us as they approached.

"What friendly people!" I laughed, flashed them and waved back. Then, at forty mph we turned a corner.

In the UK, and indeed most of Europe, signs some distance from the actual span mark low bridges, to allow tall vehicles to find an alternate route. The first sign I saw for this bridge was attached to the keystone. It marked the height in meters, and was some half a meter lower than the trailer. I had no time to brake, no time at all, it was just upon us. So I steered for the centre of the bridge and ducked. To this day I have no idea why I ducked. Possibly I was trying to get the entire vehicle to duck, or at least slouch slightly. And who knows, maybe it worked, for the trailer actually went under the bridge without hitting it. The driver of the coach, which had stopped on the other side of the bridge to allow me through, winced, and held his hand up, fingers held maybe an inch apart. Through all of this Echo sat back, blithely unaware of the potential disaster we had just avoided purely by chance.

I swallowed, and stopped at the next lay-by, to check on the map whether I could expect to come across any other 'surprise' bridges. Thankfully there did not appear to be further surprises, and so I set off again. The flashing orange light on the dashboard informed me that I would have to stop for fuel shortly, and as if by divine intervention, there ahead was a Shell fuel station. The fact that it was a Shell garage meant that I could use our Shell diesel card and would not have to use real money, which meant I could possibly have enough cash left to buy food. So I pulled in to the station, up to the pump, and stopped the engine.

I put about eight hundred litres of fuel in the tank, and went to the cash desk and paid, received the complementary cup of coffee, then headed back to the truck, climbed in the cab, handed Echo her coffee, put the key in the ignition, turned it, and **CLICK**....

CLICK is not the sort of sound you want to hear when you have a 38 tonne truck parked next to what seemed to be the only diesel pump in all of the north of Portugal. I tried a few more times to coerce the Iveco into starting. Nothing. A queue formed behind me.

Echo and I returned to the cash desk and she explained that the truck had broken down. The girl behind the counter looked at the queue, and demanded that I push it clear of the pump. Through the medium of Echo's translation I explained that as the rig weighed nearly thirty-eight tonnes, my pushing it was not an option. Then the gentleman in the flat hat who was paying for his fuel looked up and spoke to Echo. She chatted with him for a while then turned to me.

"He says that he owns an HGV garage and parts place down the road, and would you like him to have a look at the problem?" I agreed that I would, and he wandered outside, clicked the key a few times, then crawled under the front of the truck. A few minutes later he emerged, rather the worse for dust and grease, and spoke again to Echo. She blushed slightly. "He says your starter engine is…erm…broken"

I looked at her closely. "Okay, he says it is fucked!" she retorted. "He says that he has one at his yard, which he can fetch and bring here and fit, if you'd like to go with him?"

I quickly rang Mr Boss, who predictably got irritable when the concept of his having to spend money was suggested. I explained that the alternative was that the garage gets the vehicle moved onto the road, the local police then tow it away and he'd have to pay for all the charges, as well as the repair. He reluctantly agreed, so long as I could keep the price down.

The gentleman in the flat hat suggested I accompany him to his yard, help him retrieve the part and the tools, whilst Echo remained with the truck. We climbed into a Peugeot 405 pick-up truck and set off.

My first concern was that when I put my feet on the truck floor they kept going. I looked down, and most of the vehicle had no floor in it, simply a huge hole, straight on to the roadway, edged in a lacework of rust and worn out steel. This was awkward, as I am fairly tall, and I had to spend the trip actually clasping my knees to my chest lest I accidentally forget and put my feet down, at which point they would have been snapped off when they hit the road.

My second concern was that whilst there were seatbelts fitted to the vehicle, the bit where the buckle fitted would have been attached to part of the floor that was no longer there, and so rendered the whole restraint system useless,

Neither of these problems would have been quite so bad were it not for the third, and largest concern. Portuguese drivers obey the letter of the law, and of the highway code. Now, it says in the code that the only time that it is safe to overtake a vehicle is when you can see nothing coming the other way. Following this to its logical conclusion, the very safest times to overtake would be, say, at the brow of a hill, on a very tight bend, or when there is already a vehicle trying to overtake the one you are passing. On each of the above occasions you can see nothing, at all, and it must, by definition, be safe.

I think that biting your nails is a disgusting habit. Even under the most extreme stress I do not bite my nails. I have to tell you now that the only reason I have nails today is because I dare not release either my knees or the back of the seat long enough to put finger to mouth, or I would have chewed my nails down to my wrists! Merciful heavens, the pick-up may have been rusty, but it flew. I don't think I saw the speedometer drop below 120 kph for the entire trip. And I include driving into his yard and up his drive into his garage!

I must have looked unwell to the man in the flat hat, for he ushered me in to his house, which was huge. There he produced a cup of steaming black coffee and then disappeared. Before I could finish the coffee he was back, bearing an Iveco starter motor and I was shepherded back to the 405. Being prepared for what followed made me no more relaxed and I was a quivering mass of nerves by the time we returned. I could not count the number of accidents we avoided by scant inches, the number of corners we negotiated purely due to the intervention of some divine being. It is not a ride I would care to repeat anytime soon.

Back at the fuel station, the staff had put out signs that directed all the diesel-fuelled vehicles into the station from the other side. This was not useful for people who had cars with a fuel cap on the opposite side of the car to the pump, and I could see that some people were getting frustrated. The man in the flat hat got out of his car, greeted several of the frustrated customers by name, and set to work. His arrival somehow gave legitimacy to the idea that we were in fact broken down and the tension evaporated. Echo brought me a cup of coffee out, and we watched and waited. Waited a surprisingly short time, as it happens. Within twenty minutes the man in the flat hat emerged from under the truck, wiped his hands and wandered over. He spoke to Echo.

"He says, there you go, it is fixed," she said. I looked at him, and at the truck, and realised the scam. He claims to have repaired it, gets payment, and I, the foreign muggings, pays him, he drives off, and lo, he has refitted the same problem starter motor. I shook my head at him, my face radiating disbelief that he should take me, seasoned trucker that I am, for some kind of fool. I wandered over to the truck, threw the door open, turned the key...*ROAR* ... she started on the button.

After I paid the man in the flat hat the bill, which turned out to be the equivalent of about thirty five pounds, I explained to Echo my thoughts. She spoke to the counter staff, and one of the men vouchsafed that the man in the flat hat was well known for being the most efficient mechanic for miles around. If he said he could fix it, he could fix it. I was suitably ashamed for thinking that he was a crook. At that moment I realised that Portugal had become as much a favourite country as Spain in my heart.

The Old Heave Ho

The main requirement of a successful transport company is economy. Miles travelled with an empty trailer are miles that do not pay. It makes sense, then, to arrange for a return load to be available as close as possible to the point where you have delivered the last load. Mr Boss had an interesting variation on this idea, which often required his drivers to cross each other's paths, backtrack, sidetrack...there were days when you would swear that you just saw yourself heading in the other direction...

Having got the truck started we continued on our way to the delivery site. In the blazing heat of the mid day sun I stripped the canvas off the trailer and a large but antiquated crane trundled out and within two hours the trailer was relieved of its load of metal RSJs that were destined to become a new warehouse. Another hour had the sheet replaced, I borrowed a phone and called my agent. He had bad news for me. I was unlikely to get a reload until the end of the week, as the usual way of working in Portugal was to manufacture like crazy all week until Thursday, then load for export of Friday. This meant that I would have to spend the week parked on the beach. Oh deary me!

The rest of the week passed in a haze of sun, sea and s...angria. Echo and I enjoyed ourselves and each other, in a horrific display of wanton carnal frenzy. Okay, I admit, my memory may be a little hazy about that, but that is the way I chose to remember the week, and I was there, and you were not. Eventually, however, Friday dawned and saw us heading for a side street in Porto and a reload of cloth. Customs clearance swiftly followed and before I left the TIR park I checked with my agent again. He told me that I had to divert to Jerez for a top-up load of car wiring harnesses. One of the other drivers who had parked on the beach with us was heading in the same direction and consulted his map. He decided that it would be simpler to take the back roads once we re-entered Spain, rather than taking the motorway. As he'd volunteered to lead I agreed to follow and save myself the effort of navigating. In retrospect this was not a good idea.

For the first hour the trip was remarkably uneventful. The minutes and the miles passed without incident and it looked as if the trip was settling down into normality again. Then the roads began to narrow, become more winding, become more…rural. Suddenly we were winding up hills along narrow tarmac byways, crawling through villages which would, under other circumstances, be incredibly attractive. Sadly I had no time to watch and admire, as I was rather more focused on leaving the scenery where I found it. Then we stopped.

Parked on a hill, balconies scant inches from the sides of the trailer, our forward route was impeded by a John Deere tractor parked outside a tapas bar. We could not retreat the way we came, as it would be just about impossible to reverse down the hill round the blind corners. And then, in my mirrors I witnessed the arrival of The Law. Okay, he tried, but there is something less than imposing about someone in full Guarda Urbana uniform, even when he has a gun on his belt, when he turns up on a moped. At first he wanted, nay, demanded, that we reverse out of the village, but Echo managed to convince him of the impossibility of the task, so he approached the tapas bar in search of the owner of the tractor. After fifteen minutes Echo and I also looked in the bar, and discovered the Guarda, beer in hand, chatting to the locals. I caught his eye and he shrugged, grinned and compelled his companion to leave the bar and move the obstructive agricultural equipment.

Our route unimpeded we once again set off. Or rather, we didn't. The trucks, having been parked on the tarmac in the sun for about half an hour had sunk into the road, and efforts to extract them merely caused them to roll up the road surface into a petroleum-based version of a swiss roll. It was, therefore, fortunate that the driver of the tractor had parked scant yards from where we sat, slowly melting into the roadway. A chain was acquired and the tractor provided us with a tug. With one bound we were…stuck. As the road bore to the right our progress was blocked again by the large, blooming and beautiful flower boxes that overhung the balconies of all the houses up the main street. Although we could navigate between the bare balconies, the flower boxes made progress impossible. And so the Guarda Urbana, by now merry with good cheer and Cerveza, happily knocked on each and every door requesting that the flower boxes be briefly removed to allow us to bugger off.

By this time I was getting a bit of a headache and when we finally reached a road that did not look as if its life ambition was to become a cycle path, I bade farewell to our companion and located a shop where I could purchase pain killers and a cold drink to wash them down. Whilst I was there I rang Mr Boss, who informed me that the load had been cancelled and I was to rush over to Seville to load onions. Echo was delighted and apart from the emphasis on the *rush,* so was I. Of course, to get to Seville from where we were meant turning round and going back the way we had come…

I think I would like Seville, but I have really never spent any length of time there. I've driven close to it, round it, past it and through it, but this was the first time I was actually driving *to* it. However, first I needed a break, by law and by the fact I was shattered and so we stopped at the BP truckstop outside Seville for the night. When BP built the chain of truckstops they had in mind to charge drivers a fee for parking overnight. In the UK the drivers all nodded, sighed and paid, because we have always paid silly amounts of money to be allowed to park our antisocial vehicles on a rough, potholed piece of waste ground, and make use of shower blocks with one working shower, cold water and no lock on the door, eat food at a snack bar where a dead cat would work as an air freshener, and get lulled to sleep to the sound of passing 747 aircraft. Mainland Europe, however, had truck drivers of sterner stuff. When the Seville truckstop opened the Spanish drivers arrived, saw that they would be required to pay, laughed, and parked their trucks outside, blocking the entry. Since then the parking there has been free.

Dinner was a wonderful cold gazpacho, roast pork and seasonal veggies and a sublime sweet dessert that seemed to be made of spun sugar cobwebs and chocolate flavoured silk. Bed followed and as the temperature was, again, in the high eighties, we actually retired to bed to sleep.

First thing the next morning I again rang Mr Boss with a progress report. He was disenchanted with the fact I had the audacity to stop for the night in spite of being told that the load was urgent and yet he informed me that the urgent load itself had been cancelled and I was to go back to Jerez and collect the load that I was originally heading for. Once again we backtracked to Jerez, waving to Seville as once again I almost got to see it.

Mid afternoon saw us arrive at the industrial estate in Jerez, and the load was tracked down. Of course, the load was nowhere near ready and would not be in a condition to load until the next day. I rang Mr Boss, who decided that I had already wasted enough time by stopping overnight, the whole problem was of my making and I had to rush to Alicante to collect a load of shoes. And so, off we went to Alicante, waving, once again, to Seville as we passed it.

Alicante hove into view after a very long and probably illegal drive. I parked up at the industrial estate and found the factory unit that had the load. Although it was approaching midnight the lights were on and there was the sound of music, so I wandered in. The poor old gentleman who was stood by the conveyor belt clearly had not heard my approach and when I tapped him on the shoulder he leapt in the air, screaming a mouthful of the most basic and descriptive Spanish. After he had calmed down Echo explained who I was and what I wanted. The workman smiled, and gestured at the conveyor belt. Every so often a pair of incredibly pink shoes wobbled down the conveyor and when they reached him he took them off, deftly applied adhesive, attached them to a last and pressed the sole onto them. A hydraulic press pushed this firmly into place and then he ran a sharp knife around the sole to trim excess, wrapped them in tissue paper, dropped the pair into a shoebox and the shoebox in turn into a packing carton. This, apparently, was to be my load. He had been working, it seems, since 2pm, and in ten hours they had produced six packing cases of shoes. I needed sixty cases.

Mr Boss was not best pleased when I rang him. Apparently he had been in bed! I explained the situation, and he grudgingly accepted that perhaps I should take the rest of the day off. Bless! I promised to call him as soon as I had any further news and once again we retired to bed.

As good as my word I rang Mr Boss at 6am. Oh! Was it really only 5am in the UK? And Sunday? I explained that the load of shoes would take at least another day to complete and I could almost hear him wanting to send me back **again** to Jerez, but eventually common sense prevailed and I was told to wait for the load. Well, within two minutes the trailer was detached, and Echo and I spent a wonderful day on the beach, then at 6pm we returned and the manager of the factory informed me that the load would be ready for 6am. Wonderful! The idea that we could be heading home shortly was appealing and Echo had decided to accompany me, which was even more appealing.

On Monday morning the full staff of the factory arrived at 6am and the load was swiftly accumulated and loaded. After a speedy breakfast we set off, and after an uneventful day we stopped in a rather attractive lay-by and rest stop area between Burgos and San Sebastian, where we settled down for a good night's sleep. The best laid plans of mice and men are oft going breasts vertical, however, and our sleep was interrupted noisily at around 2am by a frantic hammering at the cab door. I opened my eyes, the curtains and the window, to be confronted by a number of gun-wielding Spaniards who quickly introduced themselves as Guarda Civil. Echo appeared at the window and a discussion followed. Echo started to shake.

The reason for her distress soon became apparent. We were parked directly behind a French-registered truck and it transpired that sometime during the night the driver had been dragged half out of his window and had his throat cut and his load stolen. I got the Guarda to sign my tachograph disc and authorise us to move the truck in spite of legally requiring having a break and we swiftly drove out of the park, not stopping until we reached San Sebastian and a secure parking area. That incident really brought the whole trip down. Echo explained that she hadn't realised the hidden perils of the HGV driving and the trip was certainly opening her eyes.

The rest of the trip to Cherbourg was fairly uneventful, and we pulled in to the ferry terminal on Wednesday morning. The boat was the Barfleur and we drove on board, had a good meal and retired to our cabins. Echo was allotted her own single cabin, being a young lady. Two other drivers occupied the cabin I was allotted, and so I took the empty bottom bunk, and a large and rather drunk Dutch driver wandered in and took the bunk above. The crossing was surprisingly choppy, given that it was mid summer and the Barfleur was a very large vessel, and before long the cabin was pitching and heaving. The other drivers and I commented on this, exchanged pleasantries, chewed the fat for a while, and settled down to catch up on sleep.

After about twenty minutes our rest was interrupted by a hoard of screaming kids running up and down the corridor outside. The Barfleur was a multi-use ferry, transporting not only trucks but cars and busses. This was unusual for Truckline, who, as their name suggests, were primarily involved in the transport of trucks, and their other vessels were both truck-only transport. On the plus side it meant that the service we received, which on the truck vessels was very good, was absolutely wonderful on the Barfleur. The fixtures and fittings were better, as the vessel was brand new, and the food was wonderful. It did mean that we had to put up with children, however.

After about 15 minutes the Dutch driver had decided that he was having no more of this interruption to his sleep, and as the kids started to stampede past the cabin again he threw open the door, shoved a meaty arm out and when he brought it back he had a rather startled looking teenaged boy clasped in his fist. I am not exactly sure what he said to the youth, but the youth swallowed, nodded his head, and when his feet were re-introduced to the floor he ran off like his life depended on it. Strangely we never heard another sound outside. Grinning, the Dutch driver returned to the bunk above mine, and shortly began to snore.

The crossing began to get really choppy, and the cabin started to pitch and drop, a most peculiar sensation, as if it was a lift in freefall. The Dutch driver said something I couldn't hear, and so I stuck my head out, and looked up, better to hear what he said. What he had said, it seems, was "Oh God, I am going to be sick." And he was. Violently and colourfully. Over the side of his bunk, which, by a wonderful coincidence, was where I had just put my head.

I mentioned earlier that the Barfleur had wonderful fixtures and fittings. I was never so pleased of this fact as I was that day, when I sampled the delights of the hot showers. Several times.

Risky Whisky

Whisky is one of the only alcoholic drinks I actually like. A drop of cheap blend in a cup of coffee can revive my flagging spirits, and I legitimise this by imagining that the boiling water drives off the alcohol. I also enjoy a glass of good single malt, but only infrequently, so a bottle I buy myself as a treat for Christmas can last well into May. However, some people are rather more focussed and a trailer load of whisky can be a target for determined thieves. As a result it is not uncommon for the load to be moved in unremarkable unmarked trailers, by sub-contract transport companies. The drivers are warned about the dangers and given the choice of whether they want to take the load or not, and are often paid a premium rate. Unless, of course, they work for Mr Boss, in which case they are told nothing...

The loading bay in Edinburgh was entirely unremarkable. It could have been any one of a hundred similar unremarkable loading bays in the area, so long as you ignored the high security fences and the number of security guards and checks you needed to actually get in. Boxes of bottled whisky were being loaded on to my trailer and the transport manager from the site came over to me with the paperwork. He pointed out the security arrangements, especially the part about only parking at secure, lit truck-stops at night, not picking up strangers and not stopping except for a clearly marked police vehicle. He explained the fate of some of the drivers who had disobeyed these restrictions and my knees began to wobble. As he continued, my dislike for Mr Boss increased. This was supposed to be a milk run, an easy trip to Austria, tipping in Vienna, reloading in Lentz, and straight home. At no point was the idea of sudden bloody death mentioned. I am sure I would have remembered!

I signed the paperwork to confirm I had received my instructions. I am sure there was a clause to state that I would pay the Inland Revenue the lost VAT for any and all bottles that failed to turn up, but by that time I was beginning to become paranoid. I re-sheeted the tilt trailer and passed the security cord through the eyelets, checking each one for damage, lest an alcoholic dragonfly managed to wheedle its way through the gap between the sheet and the trailer frame. A Gentleman in a Suit accompanied the transport manager and between them they sealed the trailer, recorded the number of the seal in a Special Red Book, checked it against the paperwork, stamped it in red, rechecked it and reluctantly handed me the paperwork. Echo and I got back in the truck and we set off for Austria.

I told myself that the truck was as inconspicuous as it was possible to be. The plain blue-sheeted tilt trailer was identical to any one of hundreds you see and promptly ignore on the motorway. The truck was totally unremarkable. There was no way a criminal could identify this wagon from any other. Unless, of course, he was being helped by someone in the company. An inside job! The more I thought about it, the more certain I was that the transport manager had a guilty face. And the customs officer, there was something about his eyes. They were too close together, too shifty. Obviously he was a criminal mastermind. And then the girl behind the desk. I am sure I had seen her getting out of a new car in the car park earlier. How could she afford this except by being part of a criminal gang? By the time I reached Scotch Corner I was getting really jumpy, seeing gunmen leaping out of every hedge, and flapping at every passing car. Echo found the whole thing quite funny, until I reminded her of the French driver in Spain who had his throat cut , at which point she became even more paranoid than I was. As a result by the time we arrived at Poole docks we were both quivering bags of nerves.

When we docked at Cherbourg we went to the customs shed and along with the customs paperwork we were given a sheet of paper to hand to any Gendarme in case we were stopped. I glanced at it, but paid it no real attention, filed it with the rest of the paperwork and set out. I was running totally legally, with a legitimate load and could see no reason why the

Gendarmes should have any reason to trouble me at all. Nothing could go wrong. Once again Murphy looked in, pointed a finger and laughed.

Cherbourg is not a good place to start if you want to go to Germany and Austria. Better to go via Calais, where there is a fast motorway that will take you all the way through, should you wish, to the Hungarian border with Austria. Cherbourg requires that you take a multitude of A and B roads just to get across France. One of the first main roads was entered from Cherbourg by means of a slip road that wound down through a full 180 degrees in a tight turn. It was just barely wide enough to allow a full articulated lorry round it and it was the only place for some miles that a vehicle heading east across France from Cherbourg could join the main road network, without having to drive miles out of the way. I pulled onto the slip road, accelerated, changed gear and…the gear lever came away in my hand. This left me with a bit of a problem. The truck was now in neutral, rolling to a stop, blocking the one entry to the arterial road. Behind me were a number of vehicles, all of which were now stuck.

I got out of the truck, grabbed the hazard triangle from behind the cab and started to walk back. The drivers of the three cars and one bus saw me carrying it and got quite irate. One of the car drivers started threatening me and I tried to explain that the 'Camion en panne! Boit de vitesse en panne. Grande Problem!' Indeed the truck was broken, the gearbox was broken and it was a hell of a problem. The gentleman with the attitude problem started making threats and whilst I am not a small person I abhor violence. I'm rather good at it, but I prefer to settle problems without resorting to hitting people. To my great relief a blue Peugeot 305 estate car pulled up behind the bus. Emblazoned on its flanks was the word GENDARME, the blue and orange lights illuminated and two French law officers came to see what all the excitement was about.

At this point Echo appeared, brandishing the piece of paper that the customs officers had given me. I explained to the officers that the problem I had was genuine, and that as soon as I had put the warning triangle out as required I would see if I could repair the fault or have to call for an HGV breakdown company. He was fairly relaxed and happy about this, then Echo handed him the paper. He glanced at it and the reaction was both immediate and impressive. His gun came out of the holster, his partner ran for the car and the radio and I wet myself. I looked again at the paper and this time tried to work out what it said. I understood the words, but even trying to untangle legal jargon in English is tricky. I had to do it whilst fettered by the fact that I didn't actually recognise many of the words. "This vehicle is carrying un-bonded alcohol of high value. If you should stop this vehicle please escort it to a secure compound as your first duty, before carrying out any other work. In the case of the vehicle breaking down please provide it with adequate security to prevent the theft of un-bonded spirit"…or words to that effect.

Adequate security, in this case, consisted of a Renault van full of Gendarmes in combat fatigues and with a huge arsenal of firepower standing around looking really threatening whilst I tried to repair the gearbox. The fault was apparent as soon as I had tilted the cab forward to gain access to the greasy bits. A small metal pin held the gear-stick itself to the selector mechanism and this had corroded and snapped. Although I didn't have a repair part, I had a small bolt that would, if I drilled the hole slightly larger, fit a treat. Carefully I started to drill and before long had the hole enlarged. Predictably, however, the largest drill bit I had was just fractionally smaller than the bolt, and so I decided to drift the bolt in with a hammer.

The sun was slowly setting, the whole place was fairly quiet, and maybe twenty-five armed and jumpy men surrounded me. Echo was talking to one of the Gendarmes, The temperature was falling, the repair was taking longer than I wanted or expected, and the armed guards were getting restless. In retrospect, breaking the silence by striking something with the resonance of a church bell with a hammer was not one of my better ideas. We will draw a veil over the next minute and thirty seconds, but when the excitement ended I was lying on the ground some distance from the truck, and some further distance from the hammer. My face was pressed into the tarmac by a large boot and somebody was trying to remove my earwax with the barrel of a rifle. Every muscle in my body went rigid. Except one. In that position I mused that it was probably no bad thing that I had brought several changes of underwear. I had a feeling that on this trip I may need them.

The kindness of strangers

One of the problems with working for Mr Boss was the fact that he had a habit of regarding bills that were sent to him as begging letters, whilst bills he sent out were sacrosanct. This meant that on occasions we would be warned not to frequent a certain fuel station, or avoid a particular tyre repair company. On occasions he owed so many tyre companies money that he had to keep taking wheels from trucks parked in the yard to get other trucks through their MOT. Occasionally he didn't bother, and on more than one occasion I discovered that the truck I had been driving for him was actually un MOT'd and totally illegal. Once I spent three weeks driving round Europe in a truck that had no MOT or tax, and was therefore technically uninsured as well. Had I known this I would have parked it up and hitched a lift back, but Mr Boss always had a plausible explanation. He was, in retrospect, a damned good liar, and I enjoyed the job to such an extent that I made it easy for him to hoodwink me. ..

After persuading the Gendarmes that I was not a threat they grudgingly removed their weaponry and boots from my person. I continued with the repairs and before too long we were able to continue. By the following afternoon the load was tipped, our nerves settled and we headed back to Linz and the reload. On the way we stopped at a Shell fuel station and I refuelled, then went into the office to pay with the Shell Eurocard. All was going well, until the cash register went *TING* and threw the card out. I tried again, and again the card was thrown out, this time with considerably more passion. The young girl behind the counter told me that the card was being rejected by Shell, so I found a phone box and rang Mr Boss.

"Bugger! I had hoped that you'd have been able to at least refuel once before they did that. I forgot to pay them. For the last two months."

So, to avoid problems I paid cash, which meant using all the cash that Mr Boss had given me for 'running money', plus about one hundred pounds of my own cash, which left me completely broke. Disheartened, and not a little angry, I set off again for the reload. As was becoming more frequent, the person in the office shrugged his shoulders and reported that he had no idea what load I was after. Once again I rang Mr Boss, to discover that the load had been cancelled, he had forgotten to tell me and the reload was actually from northern Spain. This immediately threw up a problem. There was no way the fuel I had in the tank would last me to Spain and back, so Mr Boss said he would arrange for me to meet one of the other drivers in Spain to get running money from him.

The trip to Spain went well. I reloaded just outside Barcelona and headed back to La Jonquera to clear customs and rendezvous with the other driver to get money. The other driver didn't show up. I got my customs cleared paperwork and rang Mr Boss, who informed me that the other driver had run out of fuel in Alicante and I would have to 'do my best'. I tried to explain that no matter how hard I tried, the truck would use diesel at a fixed rate and would not have enough to get me back to the UK. He informed me that this was not his bloody problem and I should stop worrying him with piddling little niggles. What was he paying me for? I explained that for the last three weeks he wasn't actually paying me, as once again the pay cheque had bounced, and he hung up.

Echo was getting rather panicky at this stage and to be honest, so was I. We headed back to the truck. Beside us was parked a Scottish truck and the driver was just climbing back into the cab. I waved and we got to chatting. I explained the problem and he volunteered to stay with us, as he too was heading to Calais. If we ran into problems he would at least be there as transport so we could just abandon the truck and get home with him. Off we set.

We stopped at noon for a meal, he cooked on his fuel tank and me on mine. We chatted, smoked and got to know each other. When we had finished Echo decided that she would spend the afternoon in his company, so that he would not be lonely…

When we stopped for the night I was beginning to think I may just be able to pull off the trick of getting home on the diesel I had in the tank. I'd started to play that mental game you do under these circumstances. 'Well, I've done one hundred miles and the fuel gauge has moved this far. If I can get to here and the needle has only moved to here, then I should be able to get **here** before the needle gets to half way. If that happens then I can get to St Omer before the needle gets to a quarter and thus be able to get to the UK before I ran out'. It was, of course, wishful thinking, a kind of prayer to a beneficent god, but I was feeling sort of hopeful. Echo came back to the cab and I was even more hopeful, but she collected her bag, smiled, slightly embarrassed, and headed back to the other truck. At this point I realised that our time together was over. She had moved on. I felt upset, but to be honest I had expected it. Echo was a free spirit, and had made very clear that she would be moving on at some time. It still hurt, though.

On we went, and down went the fuel gauge. It became obvious that no matter what I did I was going to run out of fuel. We went through the last peage before Calais, at St Omer, and pulled into the truck parking area. I told my friend that there was no way I could make it more than a mile or two more. I was gobsmacked when he suggested that if I could make it to the next fuel stop he would put some diesel in my truck when he refuelled his. And he did. Only one hundred litres, but it meant that he could 'lose" the discrepancy in creative accounting and I could get back to the UK. I was really grateful. I almost forgave him for taking Echo. Almost.

We parted company at Calais. That was the last time I saw, or heard from Echo. Whenever I see pictures or TV programmes about Portugal I always remember her, her happy nature and…enthusiasm. I hope she in turn thinks warmly of me on occasions.

When I arrived in Dover, I discovered that there was a flat tyre on the inside of the two tyres on the nearside of the truck. Again, I rang Mr Boss and told him that I needed someone to repair or replace it. He explained that he was 'in between" tyre repair companies at the moment, which I took to mean he hadn't paid his last contractor. Instead, I was to drop the trailer and take the truck to Birmingham where I could meet one of the other trucks and he would have a spare wheel. Once again I explained that I had a mere spit of fuel. Once again I was told to stop moaning and get on with the job…Once again, with little hope of success I set out.

By a combination of thrift and good luck I got as far as the junction to South Mimms Services on the M25 when once again the truck began to shake and judder. Rather than breaking down on the motorway I decided to pull off and try to get as far as the BP Truckstop at the services. Rattling and wheezing, the truck gasped its way onto the hardcore surface of the truck park and I eased it into a gap between two trucks, stopped the engine and got out, cursing Mr Boss, my life and my luck. The driver of one of the trucks adjacent asked what the problem was.

I explained and he said, "Well, I'll tell you what. Seeing as you're one of us, a 'Continental', what me and my mate will do is this. If you can get your truck out of here to the pumps, we'll bung in a hundred litres of fuel to get you to Birmingham. Now, if you'd just been a local, you'd have been on your own, but we have to stick together. It's the rules. You have to do the same you know?" And they did. I cajoled the Iveco down to the fuel pumps, and bless them, they put in 100 litres of fuel and paid for it. Hey guys, if you are reading this now, I have to say a big 'Thank You' for helping me out. I never did find out who you were, and you never told me, but Thanks!

As a post script to this story, when I arrived back in the yard, I explained to Mr Boss exactly what had taken place and how he only got his truck back thanks to the kindness of three truck drivers.

His only comment was, "Well, if they were so nice, why didn't they fill the tank. I'd have got another two days work out of it then!"

Truly, Mr Boss was an arse!

Truck-killed flatty puss

Sometimes it is not just human nature that can conspire to ruin your day. As an animal lover, and a lover of nature in the raw, I enjoy seeing how the animal kingdom acquits itself when in close proximity to men. However, sometimes the animal kingdom can come into far too close proximity, as the following stories may explain…

There are a lot of feral animals in Spain, and it was whilst I was on the way to La Jonquera that I encountered one in particular. I was travelling fairly slowly, and so noticed a cat, on the hard shoulder, with what appeared to be a cylindrical head. Well, you too would have stopped … Cats with a geometric cranium are things you don't often get the chance to see!

The phenomenon turned out to be a cat with its head firmly stuck inside a tin can. From the raw marks around its neck and the quantity of, um, cat poo around it, it had obviously been in distress for some little while. I had time on my hands, so attempted to help.

Whilst it was not exactly happy with me being there it didn't run, nor attempt to claw, but did make the odd growling noise, which echoed eerily through the can.

I tried for a while to ease the can over the cat's ears, with little success, when a Garda Civil Citroen pulled up on the hard shoulder in front of me, and two officers came over to see what I was doing. I thought they were going to be quite annoyed that I had stopped, but in fact they were genuinely concerned about the welfare of the cat. One of them produced some detergent from the boot of the car, and between us we applied some to the neck of the cat and the rim of the tin. Thus lubricated, ten minutes of careful manipulation saw the can come off the head of the poor animal.

Poor animal indeed. His ears were quite badly cut by the sharp edge of the tin and his neck was raw from where he'd been ineffectually rubbing at it. However he was now free. I'll never forget the look he shot us. Bear in mind this was not your average house cat, but a real wild cat, about the size of a Staffordshire Bull Terrier. He stared at the three of us, and his expression said, "I could, should I so desire, rip you to shreds with one paw behind my back. However, on this occasion I will let you live, as you have done me a small service. If, however, you should tell anyone, I will find where you live, and come, in the dead of night, and feed you your own eyeballs. So be warned!"

With that, he stuck his tail in the air, and strutted off…right under the wheels of an articulated truck. I was gobsmacked and one of the officers sat and cried.…

Gladly the cross-eyed bear

Yes, I know, but I like the title. And I'm the one with the keyboard!

The reasons for the strike are, for the purpose of this story, unimportant, although at the time they were front-page news. French truck drivers had decided, en masse, to blockade all the major routes through their country and all the ports. As a result, delivery to Spain was turning in to a real pain.

Nonetheless, I had delivered in Madrid, loaded in Seville and was on my way back to the UK. Customs had been cleared at Irun and I had just driven back in to France, when, over the CB, a voice called, "Any British truckers out there, you should pull in to the Shell petrol station, as the road to Bordeaux is closed, and we're being diverted up the back way to Toulouse and through to Bordeaux on the motorway"

Oh bum, that meant having to fork out for motorway tolls. However, I had a fuel card that allowed me to pay for toll roads, so it was not such a hardship, but it meant more delay, more expense, and as a result less profit on what was already not a particularly well paying load. At this time I foolishly believed that any savings I could make for the company, any effort to increase the profits, would reflect well in my pay rise. Pay rise? I never actually had one...

As my workmate Alan was due along this route as well, I rang him and informed him of the problem. He told me he'd meet me at the Shell station, but he was running several hours behind me and wouldn't be at the Shell station until maybe midnight. We arranged to run up to the docks together, I bid him farewell and hung up.

Rather than use the café in the petrol station, as it was a nice evening I decided to eat 'Café Camion.' I got out my cooker, set it up on the walkway behind the truck cab, and started cooking potatoes, tomatoes, ham and eggs. I hung a black bin bag on the air intake for the rubbish.

I sat in my deckchair beside the truck, looking across at the forest that surrounded the fuel station, and decided that, as the sun slowly set, the birds sang and the breeze gently stirred the leaves, that life was, on the whole, pretty damned good. I ate, washed everything up, packed away the cooker and left the bin bag ready for disposal the next day, then went and showered in the services, and retired to bed with a book. By eleven I decided that I wouldn't wait up for Alan, turned off the reading light, and fell asleep.

Suddenly I was wide-awake. The cab was dark and shaking. Someone was on the walkway giving it a hefty shove. I looked at the clock. Just after 2am. Damn you Alan, and your practical jokes. I wanted to sleep.

I leant out of the bunk, and pressed the button to lower the window in the driver's side door, stuck my head out and yelled, "Do you know what damned...time..it...is...ooer!"

It occurred to me, as I looked up, that I'd not actually seen Alan for a few months. My, how he'd changed! Instead of being five feet eight, he was well over seven feet, and by heck had he put on some weight. He really needed a shave, his breath smelt dreadful and he needed to see a dentist. His fingernails were in need of a good trim and the fur coat was really not him. Either that, or I was in fact not looking up at Alan at all, but a great big brown bear.

Alan snorted and blew steam from nostrils the size of pint pots. At that point I decided that this was, indeed, a brown bear. And I seemed to be annoying it somewhat by yelling in its face.

The problem with electric windows is that sometimes, when you want them to close, they seem impossibly slow. This was one of those times! Fortunately, after a couple of swipes at the door the bear seemed to get bored, and decided to entertain itself by trying to rip the cab off the chassis. After a while this also seemed to lose its entertainment value, and the bear went quiet. I, in turn, started to breathe again, and very quietly crept back into my sleeping bag, and hid under the covers, because as everyone knows, 15 tog of material will even fend off the axe-blows of a maniacal psychopath, so should be fine against a bear.

Eventually I fell into a troubled sleep, filled with images of teddy-bears with grudges, and soon it was morning. I was a little wary about leaving the cab, but eventually a few other truck drivers started to surface and amongst them was Alan. He sauntered across, then did a classical double-take as he looked at the side of my truck.

I clambered out of the cab to see what he was looking at. Attached to the air intake was a quantity of shredded plastic, and the side of the cab had what certainly appeared to be tooth marks on it. Of the rubbish that had been in the bag there was no sign. No eggshells, no potato peelings, no tins…brown bears like a traditional English fry-up! Who knew?

The story of Oh!

One of my deepest joys whilst driving was to immerse myself in the culture of the country I was visiting. Some people, however, don't so much immerse themselves as get in WAY over their heads…

It was on one of my many trips to Barcelona that I met Tim. It was common for goods that were being delivered to the North East of Spain to have the customs clearance processed at a place called Zona Franca, on the sea front in Barcelona. It was also fairly common practice to arrive there either on a Friday night or Saturday morning, ready for clearing customs on the Monday. This meant, of course, that you had the best part of the weekend to yourself in the city.

Tim was an interesting character. Well over six feet in height, blonde haired, broad and muscular, he was ex military, although he refused to say exactly which arm of the forces he was from. He worked for a German firm, from their Italian depot. He lived in France, and drove a Swedish truck. He also drank nothing but water. No tea, coffee, fruit juices, canned drinks...nothing at all but water.

This endeared me to him somewhat, as I found it difficult to keep up with the other truckers in their usual Saturday night ritual. This ritual, played out weekend after weekend, followed a simple set of rules. Basically, you waited until 8 pm, then got a taxi to the top of the Via de Las Ramblas and returned on foot, calling in to all the bars, strip shows and clubs on the way back. My problem was that my capacity for alcohol then, as now, was virtually non-existent; so that by the time I reached the third bar I could barely remember my name.

Tim, however, had never been to Spain before, but had heard of the ritual, and decided he'd like to try it, but without the alcohol. This suited me, because although it was quite possible I had walked the length of The Ramblers, as it was known by the English truck drivers, I could not remember anything beyond the McDonalds about a third of the way down.

Now, one other thing about the Via de Las Ramblas. During the day it is the central market street and a popular tourist attraction. However, after dark it metamorphoses into the Red Light Zone from Hell. Whatever your desires, whatever your kinks, if you had sufficient pesetas you could get it at The Ramblers. It was also well known that you stayed in groups of three or more, at all times, and you took no more money with you than you were prepared to lose. A single man, especially after 'mucha cerveza', was an easy target for the many pick-pockets or street thugs who lay in wait for unsuspecting foreign victims.

Common practice was to take out maybe 2,000 pesetas, then wrap your wallet in cling film, put it on the ground, and park your truck's front wheel on top of it. That way if your cab got broken into, a not uncommon occurrence, then your currency was safe. This had worked for years, until one occasion when a Dutch driver got back to his truck to find it up on bricks, and his money and both front wheels missing...

The Ramblers was also where various...um...night-staff plied their trade. Purveyors of The Oldest Trade, Ladies of the Night, Seamstresses (hem hem), Women of Negotiable Infection, call them what you will. Prostitution was rife. Young, old, pretty, pretty ugly, well dressed, shabbily dressed, undressed...it was all rather confusing, really. And the confusion didn't end there, as Tim was about to find out.

I will confess now to having a real soft spot for San Miguel. As I have already mentioned I am not by any means a big drinker. However, San Miguel was easily available over there, cheap, and I enjoyed the flavour. It was actually good as a thirst quencher. It was also quite 'more-ish', and as we went from bar to bar, heading back towards Christopher

Columbus' Column, I was getting more and more drunk. My truck would be parked up for two days, I could not drive, and therefore could let my hair down.

As you approach the beach along the Via de Las Ramblas, you reach The Column. This is Barcelona's answer to Nelson's Column, and it was also known to seasoned 'Ramblers' as TV Corner. And I should point out here and now, there was not a television in sight....

I was, by this time, having considerable difficulty remembering how to walk, and I mentioned to Tim, who was, of course, stone cold sober, that I would be getting a taxi back to Zona Franca, and for his own safety he should do the same. He was unimpressed by my warnings that, for all his size and sobriety, he would be an easy target for the muggers and other vultures who were no doubt watching our unsteady progress towards the sea. And then it happened. His eyes were filled with a thing of beauty. A vision in white. A blonde goddess. A tart. But he was smitten. (For those of you unsure of the meaning of smitten, it is, of course, an immature smit.)

By now I was grinning inanely, wobbling, and trying desperately not to piss myself. I did try, so very hard, to warn him against any rash decisions...that is to say, any decision that would result in a rash. He, however, was having none of it. No...Actually, he was considering having a hell of a lot of it. Now, I swear to god, had I been sober, I would have pointed out something that was painfully obvious to me. But I was making kitten mewling noises, hopping up and down on one leg, and unable to speak, for fear of spilling. So what I did was unforgivable. I left him to it, flagged down a taxi, and went back to my truck.

After using the traditional method of bladder-relief, that of widdling into the sea from the top of the dock wall, I staggered, rolled and hiccupped my way to my truck. In my condition there was no chance of doing anything technically challenging, like, for example, getting undressed, so I carefully found my bunk, and gently lowered myself onto my sleeping bag. After maybe twenty minutes, the cab stopped spinning and bucking and I began to believe I could make it through the night without calling upon the two favourite gods of the insanely drunk, Huey and Ralph. My eyes were regaining their ability to focus on the same object, and the roaring noise that had been filling my ears for the last hour was subsiding, waning, and resolving into the *LUB DUP* of my heart beating, which I found remarkably comforting. If I could hear it, I was not, in spite of all other evidence, dead.

And then, the sound of disconcertingly low-pitched giggling and the tippy tapping of high-heeled shoes trotting on concrete. My conscience pricked at me. Oh no, surely to gods...I pulled the curtain back from the windscreen. There, in the light of the sodium lamps of the docks, was Tim and the Blonde Bombshell.

I mentally shrugged. I had, I was sure, done my very best to tell him...anyway, time would... *SHRIEK! SMASH!*

Oh dear.....I shrugged, and went to a strangely guilt-free sleep.

The next day, at the crack of 11:30am, I surfaced, head pounding, stomach like a washing machine on spin cycle, and headed, unsteadily, for the shower block. It was, I thought, grossly unfair that the sun should be exactly the right colour to shine through closed eyelids without effort. Man, I felt rough. Then I saw the broken glass... Tim's Volvo was missing the windscreen...

Tim himself saw me, came to greet me and shook me warmly by the throat.

"You fucking bastard," he chirped, whilst trying to separate me from my breath. "You knew, didn't you!?! You ....."

I managed to draw a breath, and attempted to explain that I had tried to warn him, and he had brushed aside my concerns, a point he did eventually concede. I sat down and waited for the flashing lights to stop, for my vision to return, and the pounding in my ears to quieten down again, then asked him what had happened.

He went somewhat red, and explained that he'd taken her for a drink, then got a taxi back to the truck. He was fully intending to avail himself of her not miniscule charms and services. Their disrobing, if his torn shirt was anything to go by, was inspired more by passion than concern for tailoring, and he had partaken of, how can I put this delicately?...pleasures of the oral persuasion, which had led to a shared cigarette and then he turned the cab light on. It was at that moment that, from the point of view of the blonde, things went awry. For facing Tim was not the shapely blonde, busty lass he imagined he had seen at the Column, but a padded bra strapped to a fairly hairy chest, and, um, a very obviously excited meat and two veg. Tim was unimpressed. Tim was, it has to be said, quite massively shocked. Which is why the Blonde found that it was possible to leave a Volvo truck without ever touching the door. And Tim discovered why we called that part of the Ramblers TV Corner....

Melon Choly

Transport costs can be horrendous and companies will set out to save as much money as they possibly can. This can lead to some 'interesting' moments, as detailed here...

For all that I felt a proper continental trucker I was still very inexperienced. There are an incredible number of products being shipped from one country to another, and on this occasion I was lined up to collect my first load of fruit.

'Twas the week before Christmas and whilst all round the house rodents were getting in practice, sitting in silence, I was heading for Valencia to collect a trailer load of melons. On this trip I was to meet for the first time a gentleman by the name of Enrique, who was destined to become a good friend of mine over the years. The first encounter, however, was not to prove a promising one...

The loading bay was in a side street just off the sea front. Enrique greeted me warmly, and introduced me to the transport manager. It had already been explained to me by my agent that once loaded I had to report to a customs bay in Valencia, where the load would be inspected by a member of the Spanish civil service, who would then either grant or deny it right of exit. This was referred to as the 'Vet Certificate.' It had to be seen as fit for human consumption and of a quality that would not detract from people's expectations of Spanish fruit products. This all made sense. I understood exactly what I had to do and was happy with the whole procedure, so I was somewhat taken aback when, having witnessed the trailer being loaded, and preparing myself to re-sheet the load and get ready to leave, I was confronted by the transport manager. He uncharacteristically offered to take me for a meal whilst his men got the trailer rebuilt and sealed.

As I have already mentioned, I was still a novice and a hungry one at that, and so I accepted the offer.

After a truly Spanish meal of Jamón, Huevos y patatas frittas (ham, egg and chips…but it sounds more continental and interesting in Spanish…) we returned to the yard. There, as promised, stood the truck and trailer, sheeted, roped and with a customs seal already in place. The paperwork and Vet certificate were stuffed into the door handle of the truck. I flicked through it and it all looked legitimate (as if I could spot the difference!) and so with a warm smile I left the transport manager to his workforce, and set off back to England.

Only a few miles into the trip I decided that the fuel filter must be clogged. The truck, rather than running well, was blowing clouds of black smoke and wheezing like an asthmatic octogenarian, which was usually a sign of filter problems. I stopped and had a look. The filter appeared to be clear, but I changed it just in case. This was my only spare, and not picking up a replacement when I returned home was to prove disastrous later, as mentioned in 'Lanoline and Larceny' later in the book.

There was no noticeable difference. The truck still struggled for performance. However, I was determined not to stop unless I had to. I wanted to be home for Christmas and was going to attempt to be so. (As it happened, this would be the very last Christmas I spent at home for maybe fourteen years!)

The trip back to the docks in Boulogne was a nightmare. At the sight of a hill my wagon sighed with despair and struggled upwards, groaning and smoking, whilst behind me frustrated pedal cyclists waved their fists and rang their little bells in disgust at being so cruelly balked. Pedestrians stormed past me. Pensioners hurried by, the truck shaking in the wake of their passing. You get the picture?

Dogged determination to be home was the only thing that got me to the docks. Of course, my problems were not over, for on the other side of the water was Folkestone and all the roads from Folkestone contained a noticeable amount of up in their nature. However, once in the UK I could call Mr Boss, and if necessary, plead with him to send a replacement tractor unit.

As it happened, I was never to get as far as the roads in Folkestone.

I cannot bring myself to document fully the horror that was the crossing from Boulogne to Folkestone. The vessel appeared to be one of Noah's cast-offs. The crew ditto. I looked at the meal, which was a stew that seemed to consist of tubes of gristle marinated in cat urine, and at the bread, which could have usefully served to stop the trailers from rolling around on the decks, and then gave up and went to find my cabin and my bunk. On throwing back the sheet, however, I noticed that the bunk had a certain mobile aspect. Closer investigation revealed this to be what can best be described as mechanical dandruff. Dear lord, it was crawling with lice!Back then, to the bar area, and a complaint to the steward, who shrugged and ignored me.

A restless crossing was spent, trying to doze in a violently bucking chair, until we finally docked at Folkestone. Oh, joy of joys, there was a veritable disco presentation at the dockside. The flashing yellow beacons of the dockside trailer tugs was joined by the blue lights of the police and customs officers. Yippee! Another hold-up. Not to worry, I was pretty much legal, if you ignored the fact that my boss had paid the same money for the truck's road tax as I paid for my Allegro…

Disembarkation commenced. We were all required to form a line leading into the customs shed and from there to the weighbridge, where police officers were joined by Department of Transport officers and members of the Department of Employment. The vehicles could be checked over for road legality and the diesel checked to make sure it was not of the untaxed agricultural variety, whilst the driver's identity could be confirmed, as could the fact he, or she, was not working whilst claiming benefits. I was quite happy in all these respects, apart, as mentioned, from the road tax, which would not cause me any problems, but would inevitably lead to Mr Boss getting yet another summons. So I relaxed, happy to wait until I was called onto the weighbridge.

At that point the story degenerates into farce.

Having placed my truck in position on the weighbridge I watched the operator check the figures, do a double-take, and have words with the WPC stood beside him. She came out and asked what I was carrying. I showed her the paperwork, which stated 20 tonnes of melons. She checked the paperwork, then went to confer with a customs official, who went with her to check the customs seal that had been applied at Valencia.

After a brief discussion between the police officer, the weighbridge operator and the customs official I was asked, quite kindly, if I would drive round and rejoin the queue for a re-weighing, as there may be a temporary problem with the weighbridge.

Smiling and confirming that it would be no problem at all, officers, I complied, refraining from swearing mightily until I was out of earshot.

I was now at the tail end of a queue of about twenty trucks. Some of them were pulled over for discrepancies in paperwork or for other infringements of regulations. None, I noticed, had trouble with the actual weighbridge. What, then, could be the problem? I knew I had twenty tonnes of melons on board. I had watched it being loaded. The paperwork confirmed it. I had never taken my eye…oh dear…

It was with heavy heart and heavier trailer that I returned to the weighbridge. I knew, even without looking at the operator, that I was in trouble. The scream of laughter sort of gave it away. When the WPC approached I didn't even give her chance to speak, but asked her where she wanted the trailer parked for inspection. She indicated a small shed to one side of the terminal, and smiled.

I drove over and was joined in short order by the weighbridge officer, the WPC and a member of HM Customs and Excise. A brief question and answer session followed, the upshot being that I had just unofficially won the year's sweep, as being by far the most overweight vehicle they had pulled all year. I was, in fact, almost exactly twenty tonnes overweight. I think they could see the genuine confusion and concern on my face, and assured me that as I hadn't actually driven on a public road I had yet to technically commit an offence, apart, it was hinted, from the offence of smuggling.

We wandered over to the trailer, where the customs officer checked the seal number against the paperwork again, and checked the paperwork from the Vet. He then cut the seal, and bade me to open the trailer, which I did. My yelp of shock possibly woke everyone in the town of Folkestone.

There on the trailer were the twenty, one tonne pallets of melons I had so carefully watched being loaded.

On top of them the transport manager in Valencia had carefully placed a further twenty. In so doing he had so very nearly managed to save himself the shipping costs of an entire load of melons.

As I wandered over to the phone to call Mr Boss and get him to try and arrange for half the load to be unshipped, I wondered just how many times this trick had been pulled, and how many times it had been successful...

Christmas Turkey

By this time you would have thought Mr Boss would have sufficient self respect not to ask for favours. However he was not averse to a little emotional blackmail...

Having returned home from the debacle involving the overweight load of melons, I was all ready to enjoy a Christmas holiday. No work had been scheduled until after Christmas, so I was happy in the knowledge I would be able to spend some time home with my family.

Until 2am on December 23rd, when my slumber was interrupted by the clamour of the ringing telephone. Like a fool I answered it...

Mr Boss explained to me that Alan was stuck in Rome, due to Mr Boss scheduling him an unexpected reload from the delivery of beef he had made. As a result Alan was threatening to abandon the truck in Rome if Mr Boss could not come and help him get home for Christmas. Mr Boss explained that whilst he would dearly love to go and help one of his drivers he was due to fly out to Lanzarote with his family for a week holiday the very next morning, and as Alan and I were very good friends would I consider helping?

The look Girlfriend du jour gave me when I assented would have frozen the heart of the warmest person. She, unlike me, was able to see through his weasel words, and was not unhappy to give voice to her frustrations. I, on the other hand, was concerned more about Alan being stuck abroad over Christmas, which could not possibly be any fun.

Mr Boss originally had wanted me to get a taxi to Heathrow, but I pointed out that as, once again, his pay cheque had failed to clear, I was unable to afford to do so. Grudgingly he agreed to come and collect me, and incidentally let me have the cash that he owed.

True to his word he arrived within the hour and we left for the airport.

I was, I confess, less than surprised when at 5am on the 23rd December I found myself having to return half the money I had been given, because his credit card had been rejected when he tried to use it to buy the airline ticket. Nonetheless I found myself, less than an hour later, on a small bodied jet plane, heading for the planet Surreal.

My first inkling that I may have wandered accidentally into the Twilight Zone was when I observed that every passenger except me was female. And Japanese, And about 18 years old. And in school uniform…

The pilot's voice over the intercom informed us that although it was a foggy day the very tip of Mont Blanc could be seen through the windows on the starboard side. Almost instantly the entire right hand side of the cabin was filled with excited sailor-suited students taking pictures out of the cramped windows. As my seat was a window seat I was startled, yet somehow not entirely unhappy, to discover that my immediate eye-line was suddenly filled with cleavage.

On arrival at Rome airport I made my way to the observation window and finally spotted Alan's truck in the car park. Alan had been given the one new truck in the fleet, a Volvo FL10, and to be honest I was quite looking forward to driving it.

We met in the car park, and Alan re-affirmed that he had meant that he would abandon the truck where it was. He was very annoyed with Mr Boss and very grateful that I had turned up to help. Having actually managed to get more sleep than I had, Alan volunteered to take the first shift.

At this point, dear reader, I should explain some of the rules and regulations regarding driving HGV trucks, whether solo or 'double manned,' and the legislation regarding regular rest breaks. I should, but there seems little point, because quite frankly over the next 36 hours we blew them clean out of the water. Not, in retrospect, a clever thing to do, and not something I am proud of, but I plead youth and ignorance. As opposed to these days when I would be forced to plead old age and insanity…

I awoke as we pulled into a fuel depot about two hours north of Rome. Alan had decided that what we needed was coffee and food. The café area was half empty and festive paraphernalia bedecked the ceiling, walls and tables. We made ourselves comfortable at a corner table near the counter and Alan went to order two coffees and two prosciutto Panini. As we sat and ate and chatted a young lady came in and wandered up to the counter.

Maybe we were over tired, or she really did look as stunning as we seemed to think. Alan commented rather more loudly than was polite, that she was incredibly attractive and that if he had time he would have liked to have got to know her better. Luckily for us he was speaking English when he said it.

She paid for the fuel she had bought, and headed back to the door. As she passed us she leaned over, and in a wonderfully plummy English accent said, "I really don't think my husband would be too happy about that!" She gestured towards her car, where a well dressed, handsome and impressively large man was watching with interest. Alan's head disappeared between his shoulders as she smiled sweetly, patted him on the cheek, and left.

After a half hour break we went back to the truck. This time I got in the driver's seat and set off. Technically at this stage we were still legal. It was, however, to be the last time on the entire trip that we were.

Some names that we put on subsequent tacho discs include Mouse, Michael. Duck, Donald. Stiltskin, Rumple… had we been stopped at any stage we would have been in massive trouble. The law is not happy with falsification of tachograph disks. I believe the charge is 'using a false instrument' and probably carries a much greater punishment than breaking the driving laws. Again I have to say I am not proud of this.

The load we had on board was frozen tomatoes and as a result had to go through the same vetting procedure as the melons I mentioned previously. This was done at a beautiful place called Aosta. By this time snow was falling heavily and as we pulled into the lay-by outside the customs sheds the sun was setting, and the lights were coming on. Whilst Alan went to sort the paperwork out, I looked around. The lay-by we were parked in was usually filled to overflowing with trucks heading into and out of Italy. The customs area was not far from the Mont Blanc tunnel, and therefore usually chaotic. This evening however it was incredibly peaceful. The falling snow muffled sounds and the only interruption to the perfect tranquillity was an aeroplane practicing landings in the snow at the airfield to the right of the truck.

Alan returned and took the wheel, and we pressed onwards, up to the Mont Blanc tunnel. As we climbed we passed villages of Swiss-style chalets, little cottages, farmhouses. All of them bedecked in colourful Christmas lighting. The scene, with the snow gently falling, was magical. I felt strangely at peace. For a moment I began to imagine the birth of a child two thousand years before, in a manger, in poverty, who was destined to be...I was thrown off my seat by Alan braking the truck to a halt.

He gestured to a silver and black Volvo truck parked by a café.

Jan was a Dutch truck driver, who I first met in Aosta when I first delivered beef to Italy. Our trips meshed perfectly and we met regularly at Aosta when we came in and when we left Italy. We had become good friends. We waved to him, as he left the café and climbed into his truck, and yelled to him that we'd meet him at the boarder.

Again we set off, up the long incline to the Mont Blanc tunnel. For all that the FL10 was a new truck it was, predictably, underpowered for the job it was being asked to do. As a result we were overtaken by several Italian and French wagons on the way up. Alan turned on the interior light, and as we were overtaken by the next French wagon the driver was greeted by the vision of two crazy Englishmen who appeared to be madly cranking the truck to get it up the hill.

The Mont Blanc tunnel is a fascinating feat of engineering. At over seven miles long, it cuts through the mountain and links Chamonix with Courmayeur. Many years after this job it was to be the scene of a massive, devastating fire in which sadly thirty nine people were to lose their lives. At the time, however, it was simply an awe-inspiring drive from Italy to France.

By this time both Alan and I were beginning to feel the effects of fatigue, and it was then we discovered that we were both massive fans of Monty Python. The journey through the tunnel was accompanied by two insanely giggling Englishmen reciting the Dead Parrot sketch, passages from The Holy Grail and The Life of Brian. Words cannot express how happy I am now that nobody was listening that night...

We emerged into more falling snow. The scenery, once again, was breathtaking, and enhanced by the incredible sculpture on the French side, which, to my tired brain resembled a glass of wine being proffered to all who passed by.

Parking up we headed to the Bureau De Change and exchanged our Lira for French Francs. It does seem strange now that this in no longer necessary. The Euro has somehow robbed us of this wonderful distraction.

As we sat under the shelter of a canopy, watching the snow gently falling and drinking yet more coffee, Jan emerged from the tunnel and pulled up alongside us. As Alan went to get us all some coffee Jan and I chatted. I was beginning to get unhappy with Mr Boss's cavalier attitude, and expressed my opinion. Jan, however had a more relaxed approach to life.

"My friend, you take life too seriously. Who knows what tomorrow may bring. We are only alive until we die. When it is your time to go, you go. That wasn't your time. Relax!" He patted me companionably on the back, spilling my coffee in my lap.

We sat and chatted, drank more coffee, smoked a cigarette, and then departed. I promised Jan I would see him later. I never did. He died on the 30th December when his truck slid off the 'ski-slope' as he headed towards Mont Blanc from the French side.

Neither Alan nor I can remember a lot about the rest of the journey home, until we reached Calais, where the weather was blowing an absolute storm. Apart from us and one other truck all the vehicles were cars and motorbikes.

We boarded the ferry, and headed for the driver's rest room, intent on getting some hot food, for we had survived on one toasted bacon sandwich. However, when we got to the drivers canteen it was closed! We knocked, possibly more forcefully than was needed, and the manager stuck his head out.

He was somewhat worried when we told him we were hungry. The crossing, he informed us, was at least gale-force eight. We would not want to eat. We'd never keep it down. And besides, they hadn't cooked anything.

We complained bitterly. We bargained. He would make us each a huge plate of bacon sandwiches, if we would please piss off and be sick elsewhere. We readily agreed.

Oh, my good friends, what a crossing that was. It is strange, but neither Alan nor I suffer from Mal de Mer. However, it soon became apparent that the vast majority of the passengers were unhappy in the extreme that they were in a comparatively small ship, bobbing about in a comparatively large sea. I have to say that the over-riding hue was green, with hints of purple.

Okay, I will admit that it may have been my idea, but one way or the other it was decided that the best way to help these poor broken people was to offer, and indeed show them the bacon sandwiches. Sadly, as a medical experiment, it was a total failure. Nobody was miraculously cured. Several of them wanted to kill us, but were unable to as they were indisposed. Look, we were very tired, and living purely on caffeine and adrenaline. I would offer my humble apologies to you, except at the time it was incredibly funny. And I am a bad bad man!

Finally, we arrived back at the docks. Much to our surprise and delight Alan's cousin was there. He'd heard about Mr Boss' treatment of us, and had come to the ferry to meet us, and drive the final leg home. We cleared customs, climbed into the cab and set off. Wanting to hear all about the trip, Martin was instead serenaded for the entire journey home by the sound of snoring in two-part harmony.

And just for the record, Alan got home at just ten minutes to midnight on December 24th. Happy Christmas!

Gastric Phew

*After the debacle that was 'Melon Choly' I next saw Enrique in the early summer of
the following year. In fairness he was unaware of his manager's actions and was genuinely
upset at what had happened. The cynical amongst you may say that is at least partly due to
having to pay compensation, but I think he was genuinely upset at having a mark against his
reputation. Over the years, as I got to know him better, my belief in this was reinforced. He
was, in my opinion, a rarity, an honest businessman...*

I'd unloaded some British strawberries at the Valencia fruit market and Enrique, the
man in charge, had invited me out for a meal, as recompense for my being dealt a low blow
on our last meeting. He'd been waxing lyrical about the paella at the local restaurant and in
spite of my protestations that I really did not like seafood, tonight I was going to enjoy a meal
fit for a king. After all, he argued, how could anyone not like seafood?

After a glass or two of a very nice local beer and some tapas, the waiter arrived at the
table with the dish. In a bed of rice and vegetables lurked un-named and un-nameable pieces
of some poor deceased sea creature. And not, by the smell, recently deceased. Things with
suckers seemed to be eating the rice, whilst bits of green were definitely taking the peas...

In spite of my continuing protestations, Enrique served me a huge plate of the gunk,
and a similar portion for himself, then sat and watched. I really like Enrique and didn't want
to hurt his feelings, so I tucked in. Hmm...

It was not as bad as I first thought.

It was, in fact, ten times worse.

Bitter, slimy, undercooked in places, overcooked in others…Enrique looked on, paternally, proud and pleased that I was eating.

After I'd eaten about half, he started on his, and then croaked, and spat it out, accompanying the spitting with loud yells of very earthy and unhappy Spanish. Apparently the food was dreadful, and worse, it had gone off. I, being a non seafood eater, had simply assumed the awful bitter, gritty, slimy taste and texture was an acquired taste. Turns out I was wrong.

Enrique was hugely apologetic. Not only had his workers treated me badly the last time I was there, but this time in his effort to placate me he had inadvertently tried to poison me. I excused myself, found the nearest Gents, and communed briefly with the good lords Ralph and Huey.

We left the restaurant and Enrique insisted on getting me another drink. I managed to persuade him that as I was driving early in the morning I would only have a coffee, and after that I retired to the truck, only to discover a note on the windscreen.

Apparently my reload had been rescheduled and I had to be in the outskirts of Gerona in four hours. Whilst I had the time to do the run I really wasn't feeling any too well, but a reload was a reload, so I set off.

To be honest the drive wasn't too bad for most of the 400 or so kilometres. However, as I got to the peage (the toll-road payment booths) to get off the motorway at Gerona, I felt what could best be described as ominous rumblings from my stomach. I still had a way to go, as the paper mill wherein I had to reload was in a village called St Joan Les Fonts, up in the hills.

The rumbling of my stomach was getting almost as bad as the rumbling of the tyres as I negotiated the twisting road as it climbed into the hills. Oh lords, I really did not feel too well. Not nauseous, but certainly a lot less than healthy. I felt…sort of bloated, and windy, and…oh crikey, I really needed the loo. NOW!

I shot into the factory at reckless speed, stopped the truck in the middle of the yard, made stupid hand gestures to the rightly concerned security guard and double-timed to the toilets.

Some while later I emerged, pale and sweating. Apologising to the guards I put the truck on the requisite loading bay, and then, hells bells! Back to the loo.

Let me draw a veil over the rest of my time there, except to say it was a long and lonely night. And there were 47 rivets in the toilet door. 166 tiles on the walls. 43 badly written pieces of graffiti. Seven of them in English. There were four rolls of toilet roll in the cubicle when I first arrived. There were two and a little bit when I left.

Eventually, maybe a little after three in the morning, I felt safe enough to get some sleep, as I really had to leave the factory at 6, to have any chance of getting to Cherbourg on time for my booking. When the alarm went off at 5:45 I woke feeling drained, in every sense of the word, but not too bad to drive. After all, I'd done this job, and this trip, dozens of times before. What could go wrong?

As it happened, what could go wrong was waiting for me at the top of the hill as I left the factory. A notice from the Guarda Civil warning of speed and vehicle checks. I was okay, of course. Everything was legal and above board. The trailer and truck were well in weight, and Mr Boss had serviced the trailer just before I came out. At that point alarm bells and klaxons totally failed to alert me to the incongruity of that thought.

I set off down the long winding hill towards Gerona, the motorway, France, and home. After a few minutes the rumblings started again, although in a far more muted and less threatening manner. So long as nothing upset my composure I would be fine. There were plenty of service stations on the route, so I had no problems.

Until I touched the brakes and nothing happened.

With air brakes, as fitted to articulated trucks, the brakes are actuated by compressed air. When you learn to drive HGVs, unless you have had previous experience of the power of these things, you will stick your driving teacher and any other people in the cab to the windscreen every time you apply the brakes for at least the first two days. As a result you instinctively feather the brakes. I feathered.

The one thing you desire most when you touch the brake pedal in a fully loaded truck is braking effort. You want to feel the reassurance of 38 tonnes of vehicle being slowed by friction material being pressed against brake drums. You really do not want to hear a worryingly cheerful whistling noise, as if the brake pedal has suddenly become an annoyingly chipper cockney chimney sweep straight out of Mary Poppins.

I was, therefore, not very happy when I pressed the pedal, to be greeted by Dick Van Dyke's cheery whistle and no retardation whatsoever. This was a whole world of worry. In front of me was a steep descent on winding roads, a stupidly busy peage, then most of Gerona, and finally the sea. If I could find no way of slowing my descent I was in danger of visiting each of the above, in order, at increasing velocity, until I hit something that was big enough to provide its own braking effort, at which point it was almost certain that it would be me that got broke…

A few seconds of panic gave way to ice cold clarity. I am, I think, blessed with the ability to think a problem through without worrying too much, dealing with the problem and then panicking afterwards, when it is less likely to get in the way.

I killed the ignition, which stopped the fuel going in to the engine and turned it into an eleven litre brake. This served to slow the truck a little, but still gave me power for the steering and air for the truck brakes, which should work even if the trailer brakes are under the impression they are part of a set of bagpipes.

Next I started to carefully feather the handbrake. This would, I hoped, allow the truck brakes to work independently of the trailer brakes, and stop the air leak from draining my air tanks and leaving me with no chance of stopping. All things considered, I thought I had everything pretty much under control.

As long as I didn't need to stop in a hurry, I should be fine. So long as I could just maintain my speed and slow gradually, I'd be great. And after all, I'm half way up a mountain. What could possibly stop me?

Do you remember me mentioning the notice from the Guarda Civil?

About half a mile in front of me, at the side of the road, was a Guarda Civil inspection site. In the lay-by two Citroen police cars, two motorcycles and a large green Portakabin. On the road....briefly I was of the opinion Laurel and Hardy had signed up as Spanish Law Enforcement officers. One was…well, on the large size, whereas the other looked as if a uniformed pipe cleaner had put a flower pot on its head.

I sounded my horn, in the universal language of distress. SOS. Three long. Three short. Three long. It would have been spectacularly successful, too, had I not turned the ignition off earlier, thus disabling the horn…

Stan and Ollie seemed remarkably sanguine, given that they were being rapidly approached by 38 tonnes of truck that didn't seem to be slowing. I pulled the handbrake lever harder. The smell of burning brake lining got noticeably stronger, but my speed didn't decrease. Smoke was now billowing from the wheels, and Stan and Ollie were looking worried. Ollie stepped to the side of the road, but Stan, who I could now see was barely out of nappies, stood in the road, assured of the powers his hat and uniform bestowed upon him. He held his hand out in front of him, palm up, in the well recognised sign meaning 'STOP!'

But I couldn't.

Oh help! I was going to kill a Spanish Police Officer. They don't like it when you do things like that. They get remarkably unhappy. The police officer you kill is unhappy too, I should imagine, but on the bright side that feeling is transient. Maybe that isn't such a bright side…

At the very last moment Ollie reached out, grabbed Stan by the over-large lapels of his khaki and green overalls and by main force dragged him into the side of the road. I shot past, wheels aflame, at about 45 miles per hour. Not massively fast, but by gods I had the inertia to flatten a block of flats!

It must have taken me about another two miles to stop, by which time the truck wheels were actually alight and the tyres burning. Also by this time Stan and Ollie, and a couple of police motorcycles, had caught up with me, and two of the motorcycles had got in front and did a sterling job of clearing the traffic. Although at 6:15am there isn't a lot of traffic about. Just me, in a truck with 20 tonnes of paper and burning wheels, two police motorcyclists, Stan and Ollie.

As soon as I had come to a stop, more by luck than judgement in a lay-by, the two Garda Civil officers attacked the burning wheels with remarkably effective fire extinguishers. Very soon after that the fire brigade arrived and made very certain that the wheels were not likely to relight. They had rightly guessed that as I was loaded, and heading downhill from St Joan, that I would have paper on board.

I climbed down out of the cab, shaking, and went to see Stan and Ollie. I wanted to apologise to Stan for nearly turning him into a Khaki speed bump, but before I could speak Ollie asked if I was all right. He was the senior officer and looked a little sheepish.

When I had convinced him that apart from being shaken I was fine, he started speaking very quickly, so I was having difficulty understanding him. Whilst I speak Spanish better than many Brits, it is transport focussed, and whilst it has improved a lot since then I still have difficulty following the language when spoken rapidly. I could make out that Stan had done something that really he shouldn't have done and Ollie hoped I would see me way clear to realising there were "extenuating circumstances." Or possibly "consenting motorcycles," although that seemed less likely.

He took me round to the back of the trailer.

At first I could see nothing wrong.

Then I noticed…the back and side of the trailer had holes in.

Lots of small holes.

Holes that you would get, perhaps, if in a fit of pique you had discharged a machine gun at a passing truck?

Holes that I could see started maybe about a foot behind where my head would be were I sat in the truck. Stan had, indeed, been piqued. And armed…

My stomach lurched. Not many minutes later I was so glad I had 20 tonnes of paper on the trailer. I was going to need it…

Kidnapped

The incident with the Guarda Civil was not, sadly, my only encounter with people with firearms. Much like London buses, you don't see one for an age, then two come along at once!

There are some questions that need to be asked, such as "I don't wish to alarm you, but does anyone here know how to fly a 747?" or "Could you please take your foot off my oxygen pipe?"

There are some that really need not be asked, such as "Can I get you a drink?" or "I'm a member of the opposite sex who finds you both intellectually stimulating and physically attractive. Would you like to come back to my place?" Although, to be fair I've never heard any of the above...But I live in hope of one day hearing the last one...

There is one question I was asked, however, that I found incredibly stupid, but was really in no position to say so.

Delivering beef to the American air force bases in Italy and Sicily had become a regular run for me, and I'd gotten into the habit of stopping at the same truck stop every time I came. This was, in hindsight, not a good idea. A truck load of prime Scottish beef is worth a lot of money and if it can be secured for little effort it is going to attract the attention of undesirables.

So it was at around 3am that I was awoken by the sound of urgent hammering on the side of my cab. In a daze I struggled free of my sleeping bag, wound down the window and stuck my head out, only to meet the barrel of a gun coming the other way! Hmm...I recognised the weapon as a Browning 9mm, a gun I had frequently fired at shooting ranges, but strangely I couldn't remember the barrel being quite as large as it suddenly appeared. Then came the question, asked in incredibly good English, and so very politely.

"Excuse me. Pardon the interruption, but would you mind if my friends and I were to borrow your truck for a few hours?"

Well, given that my sinuses were currently being cleared by several inches of blued steel, and the smell of gunpowder was overpowering my senses, I could only answer one way.

"Do, dad is fide. Helb yourselb!" I jabbered.

The gentleman invited me to get back into my sleeping bag, draw the curtain and go back to sleep, and above all, not to worry. They really did not want to hurt me.

It occurred to me that they hadn't said they were not going to hurt me, merely that they did not want to. I got the feeling that they would be ever so upset, but would do so anyway. Go back to sleep? Hah!

The truck shook as several heavy bodies climbed in. Did I say bodies? Oh dear!

Then the same voice rang out.

"Sorry to bother you. Are you asleep?"

I indicated, via the medium of squeaks and chattering teeth that I had not reached the blessed state of sleep.

"Oh, that is good. I don't suppose you'd be so kind as to let us have the keys, would you?"

The curtain twitched open, and the barrel of the gun appeared. Not knowing what to do, I hung the keys on it, and it disappeared again. The chap laughed.

"That's the spirit!"

The truck was started, and off we drove. There was the occasional direction being given in what I assume was Italian, but apart from that the journey was in silence, apart from the booming of my heart.

The sun rose and my spirits sank. We were apparently driving over fairly rough terrain, maybe a farm track, then suddenly the cabin went dark, and the sounds echoed as we pulled into a large enclosed space.

"Do us both a favour, my friend, and stay put. I'm leaving Luigi here with you. He doesn't speak English, but has been known to get annoyed if people don't do as he wants. And what he wants most of all is for you to stay there, stay quiet and stay…..safe…"

For about an hour I lay on the bunk, listening to what must have been several people manually unloading the trailer. Then the cabin lurched again.

"Okay, soon be over. Won't be long and you won't have anything to worry about."

Oh dear merciful heavens. An outright threat!

The truck started and off we set again. We drove for maybe another hour, but for me it seemed like a lifetime and at the time I was absolutely convinced it was. Finally, with a hiss of airbrakes, we stopped.

"Okay, what I would like you to do now is get out of the cab and kneel down by the door. Do not, and I cannot stress this enough, DO NOT try to look for us. I will be standing beside the truck and if you so much as glance at me I will be forced, against my wishes, to shoot you"

I did as I was told. Hands sweaty, heart racing, and clad in white boxer shorts with hearts on them, I climbed out of the cabin and knelt down.

"Thank you. You have been a very nice passenger."

I felt the barrel of the gun against the back of my neck.

"And now we must go. I hope you are not too bitter about this. This is just a business transaction for us and occasionally someone gets hurt. No ill feelings, I hope?"

The bang, when it happened, was a lot quieter than I was expecting. In the milliseconds between the report and the numbing pain I had time to reason that the gun must have had a silencer fitted. But then I remembered seeing it, unsilenced, when he shoved it up my nose. Maybe he had a silencer in his pocket? But then, why would he use a silenced weapon when we were on a track miles from anywhere? And how come, now I think about it, am I managing to think all this in the time it takes for a bullet to enter my head? And why can I hear a car driving off? And…didn't the gunshot sound almost exactly like a car door being slammed? And am I not, therefore, kneeling on the ground on the side of a hill in Italy, wearing embarrassing underwear for no reason?

I looked up. I was being watched from the side of the road, by a small but inquisitive goat…

New Shoes

One more gun-related incident, to make three in a row, all within two months of each other. Luckily to date this was my last encounter with a firearm...

I had sat at Alicante TIR park for four days, waiting to clear customs. I had on board 20 pallets of paraquat weed killer and two 2lb bags of household sugar. Would you like to guess which of the two were causing me the problems?

Finally, however, my customs agent came trotting up with the cleared paperwork and I was free to go and deliver the load to the loading bay, a good thirty feet from where I was parked. This event would have been so much less stressful had the fork-lift driver not driven over the two bags of sugar that had been causing the hold-up in the first place...

After the shouting and recriminations had died down to an occasional curse, my agent came over and told me I had to reload shoes. He explained that he would lead me to the centre of Murcia, where I would park up and wait. And so he did.

The green space where I parked up was strangely attractive. As I have mentioned before, I have a love for Spain, the architecture and the people. There was something incredibly charming about the blocks of flats, the small shops, the children running around, the adults enjoying a relaxing drink in the tapas bars...the whole atmosphere was so relaxing. Until suddenly six small vans hurled themselves round the corner, and screeched to a halt beside my truck.

Immediately a dozen people appeared from the houses around the area and formed the only example of a genuine human chain I have seen in my entire life. As my agent arrived they were passing large boxes of shoes from hand to hand, from the vans to the trailer, where two large individuals were rapidly stacking them at the front.

Suddenly the vans were empty. They crowds vanished and so did the vans. And then, half an hour later they returned, and the situation repeated itself.

I asked the agent if I could go with him on the next trip and he willingly agreed. We sped off into what looked like a residential area, filled with ten-storey housing blocks. As we drew up to the side of the road one of the van drivers let out a piercing whistle. And I stood, stunned, watching what followed.

A window, about five storeys up, was flung open and a box hurtled out. One of the men caught it, and threw it onto the van. Another box, another catch, another load…one of the younger lads was, I swear, about three inches shorter by the time the loading had finished. The agent explained that the residents of the entire block had clubbed together and bought the equipment to make shoes for a local company. Even he had no idea why it was all assembled on the fifth floor, but it had been this way for a couple of decades and the system worked.

Next thing I knew, we were hurtling along the streets back to the truck and the chain started again.

Within three hours I was totally loaded and ready to go. I sealed the trailer, collected the paperwork from my agent, waved to the local helpers and set off for Irun.

It was about 2am the next morning when, as I was driving along a road next to the motorway, I was passed, very rapidly, by a dark green Citroen BX with blue and red lights atop. On came the lights, and the passenger signalled with his illuminated baton that I was required to pull over.

I stopped, and two members of the Ertzaintza climbed out of the car. More commonly known to truck drivers as the Redcaps, the Ertzaintza were the police force for the Basque region of Spain. I made a mental shift in gears, ditched Spanish and adopted French as my language of choice.

"Good evening sir. I have to tell you that you are not allowed on the road when there is a motorway nearby" the first of the Redcaps informed me, politely but firmly.

"Oh? I am sorry, I did not realise. Could you explain to me why that is?"

"You are carrying une charge dangereuse," he explained.

I blinked. I knew that being hit by a falling box of shoes could be painful, but surely that didn't mean I was carrying a hazardous load...

I looked at the trailer. Ah! I still had the stickers on the trailer showing it was carrying the weed killer. I promptly adopted a look of desolation.

"I am so sorry to have wasted your time. I actually only have shoes on board. Regard! Chaussures!" And I showed him the paperwork.

"Then why are you displaying the hazard stickers on the trailer?"

I explained that the over-zealous customs officer in Dover had decided that the self-adhesive stickers needed help and had sprayed glue over the trailer. I could no longer actually remove the stickers. The officer wandered over and had a go for himself. After a couple of minutes he had removed a piece the size of his little fingernail. Then his eyes lit up!

"I have just the thing!" he cried, wandered to the car and opened the boot. From a black bag he produced the biggest black felt tip pen I have ever seen. The nib was a good two inches across. He set about scribbling over the stickers with gusto, then wrote his badge number underneath each of them. Dear Gods, it was going to take me forever to get the damned trailer clean after all this. I smiled at him.

"There you go," he said, replacing the pen in the boot. "Now you have no problems!"

I thanked him, and then, in a fit of stupidity, I said "I'm afraid you have a small problem though."

He looked around. His companion looked around. "No, we have no problem that I can see!"

I pointed, in what I hoped was a helpful manner, at the rear light of his car, which was out.

He went red. He went as red as his beret. And he drew his gun.

Dear lord! Three times in two months someone has pulled a gun on me. And another Browning! What is it with Brownings?

And then he started hitting his rear light!

With the barrel of the gun!

I know from experience that a Browning can be a little on the temperamental side. If you drop one it will like as not shoot you in the foot. And here was an officer of the law using one as a repair tool!

And remarkably, the light came on before he shot either himself, his colleague or me.

"There…no more trouble. Thank you sir, and good night."

And they drove off.

I waited a few seconds before I got back in the truck, drew the curtains, and got changed…

After that, the trip back home was uneventful. I arrived in the UK, at Dover, on Sunday afternoon and checked my delivery address. Apparently I had to deliver to 29-35 Rathbone Street, the International Shoe Agency, at 8am, so I settled down for a sleep and an early start…

I knew, instinctively, that something was wrong.

Usually, when you deliver to a warehouse you do not find, at 8am, shiny chrome tables and chairs on the street, quaint bistros opening their doors to early morning power-dressed men and women, wearing suits that would have cost me my entire year's salary. They, in turn, stared in disbelief as 38 tonne truck lumbered down the cobbled street.

There, on my left, was the building. 29-35 Rathbone Street. Um...

Rather than a large warehouse it turned out to be an elegant building of quite some age. Dark stone, with an imposing dark and heavy wooden door. Something, I told myself, something was not right here.

I walked up to the door. Oh good. It appears to be a film production company. But wait, there! There's a card. International Shoe Agency. Oh...'Offices of' the International Shoe Agency.

My stomach sinking, I buzzed the buzzer. After a short while a young woman opened the door. I explained that I had some shoes for her. "Oh good! How many?"

"About twenty tonnes of them..."

"Oh...bugger"

I got the impression she was not happy as she led me up several flights of steps to the offices.

A distinguished gentleman was talking on the phone, and when he put down the handset she motioned to him.

"This gentleman here has some shoes for us. He's brought them in from Spain."

"Oh, good. How many?"

"About twenty tonnes."

"Oh...bugger!"

I could tell this was not going to end well.

The gentleman approached me, put his hand companionably around my shoulders, and yelled into my ear.

"DO YOU SPEAK ANY ENGLISH?"

"No, sorry mate, not a word!"

He had the decency to look embarrassed.

Checking the paperwork took about half an hour. Apparently I had been handed not the delivery address but the billing invoice. I actually needed to be at The British Shoe Corporation in Leicester. Oh. Good…

When I went out of the door I discovered that the local council had helpfully dropped two skips behind the wagon, so I could not reverse. This immediately made a bad job into a nightmare, for the road ahead turned right, very tight, and the same council had seen fit to put some very solid cast iron bollards along the very edge of it…

It took me two hours to manoeuvre out of there. In that time I built up a line of traffic the likes of which has only been seen since on the M25. I knocked over three of the bollards. I ripped the front step off the truck. I caused three of the local beat bobbies to quick-step out of the scene, before they got caught up in the paperwork. And yet nobody complained and I got a round of applause from the locals when I finally got round the corner. To come face to face with a foreign limousine parked just far enough across the road to make it impossible for me to go any further.

Eventually, after a further ninety minutes, I was able to escape and liberate the line of traffic so congenially stuck behind me, and I set off for BSC in Leicester. I knew they were going to be irked, as I was supposed to be there at 8 am. Mr Boss had made it painfully clear I should have to be there at 8am. So, imagine my great surprise when, having pulled in and queued at the BSC for two hours I discovered that yes, I was supposed to be there at 8am. On the following Wednesday…

Lanoline and larceny

It became increasingly clear, as time progressed, that the company for which I worked was not in the best of shapes financially. On several occasions my Girlfriend du jour rang me to tell me that my pay cheque, meagre as it was, had bounced and I had to ring Mr Boss to sort it. To start with he had the grace to sound embarrassed, but the more often it occurred the more he made it sound as if I should be grateful for a job at any cost and that I had nothing to worry about, as all I had to lose was my job, my house and my possessions. Turns out that he was in grave danger of losing his new Volvo estate car…

It was just before 3 am, in the truck park of Aire de Village Catalan, a beautiful motorway service station, just north of Spain, on the Mediterranean coast. And I was crawling very quietly under the front axle of a Spanish registered Iveco lorry. It had been a most eventful trip, ending up with me committing a petty larceny on a frosty spring morning.

It had started uneventfully enough. I had loaded unprocessed sheepskins from south Wales, for delivery to Alicante. Unprocessed sheepskins. What a nice, clinical, harmless phrase. What it meant was the skins and wool of slaughtered sheep, complete with any body fluids that may have come into contact with the fleece, and which had probably been stored for days in a warm shed. To put it bluntly, it was 20 tonnes of stink, wrapped in wool. It was possibly the second most unpleasant load I have ever had the misfortune to deal with. Maybe the third. The load in 'Something Offal This Way Comes' was one of the top three. I am not sure that I could ever bring myself to document the worst. However, this was an evil smelling load. And it dripped.

As was usual with this load, it shipped from Poole to Cherbourg, on a ship called the Coutance, a freight-only vessel operated by Truckline. As usual, I found myself being directed to reverse up the gantry, or link span, on to the top deck, as none of the crew wanted the stench in the lower hold. There was one minor problem they overlooked. Before the ship had been converted so that it could load both top and bottom decks from two separate link spans, the method of loading involved trucks driving onto the bottom deck, then being raised on to the top deck via a huge lift, and reversing into position. When the ship was modified the lift was left in place. This meant there was a 60-foot gap in the floor of the top deck. A gap that seemed designed specifically to allow leeched body fats and fluids from sheepskins to drip on to the trucks below.

Which was why, having partaken of a good meal on board and a fair quantity of wine, I was just settling into the bunk for six hours of sleep when I was rudely awakened by a cheery French Matelot. He asked, nay demanded that I move my truck from off the lift, as the smell from the effluent was making his below-deck colleagues sick. Trying to reverse a trailer across a swaying and pitching deck, in the dark, whilst pissed, was an experience I chose never to repeat. And if anyone is reading this who happened to have a lorry on the deck that night, I apologise for any dents that may have occurred…

After a reasonable night asleep, we were roused at 6am, in time for a quick breakfast and coffee and we steamed in to Cherbourg. Having disembarked, I parked the truck and went to clear customs. When I returned, I noticed mine was the only truck in that area of the truck park, all the others being huddled in a group at the other end of the docks, away from the smell. I felt as if they were all talking about me!

The plan was that I should wait for my colleague Martin to arrive at the docks, and we would swap tractor units, as I was in his Volvo at the time, and he had my Iveco. Martin was an old friend and also part owner of the company. Once we had swapped tractors he would continue back to the UK with his load of paper and I would carry on into Spain, to deliver in Alicante two days hence. It had also been decided that as another of our drivers, Alan, was shipping over on the next boat from Poole, he and I would run down together as far as Bordeaux, whereupon he would take the road to the west of Spain, and I would head east. A simple plan. What could go wrong? Murphy raised his hand with the answer...

As I have previously mentioned, Alan and I were good friends, but the nomadic existence of the trucker meant we seldom spent much time together. So it was suggested, just off the top of someone's head, that we should have a coffee and a quick chat before Martin caught the boat back at 3pm, and so we headed off to the coffee bar. Unfortunately the coffee bar also sold good wine. Just the one glass of wine each, we thought. And then we would set off, and Martin would get the boat back at 3 pm.

Well, maybe we will have a bite to eat in the restaurant in the supermarket down the road, as Martin doesn't have to worry about the boat until 3 pm.

And with the meal, maybe just one more glass of wine. And then we would set off, and Martin could catch the boat at 3 pm.

But really, the wine glasses were only small and we had just had a meal, so possibly just one more, and then we would set off, and Martin could get the boat at 3 pm.

At 4:30 pm we staggered back to the dock. Martin's truck was alone in the truck park. The ship was nowhere in sight, although to be honest, it could have been five feet away, and none of us would have spotted it, unless it had the word Vin on it somewhere. Oh dear! We were inebriated. We were tiddly. We had fallen for the wheedling words and seductive ways of that most evil god, Bacchus. Let's face it; we were pissed as farts...Only one thing to do, then. Martin could catch the 10 pm boat, but we had to, absolutely had to get on our way now. After just one more glass of wine...

Let me take a small break here, and tell you of the funniest one-sided telephone conversation it has ever been my great fortune to witness. I had come out of the Truckline offices in Cherbourg, to ring Mr Boss to verify the delivery address and let him know which ship I was catching back to the UK. The one working telephone booth was occupied by a somewhat inebriated gentleman from Ireland, and I heard:

"Boss, I missed the boat!"

Pause...

"No, boss, I missed the boat, I..."

Pause...

"Yes boss, the next boat is at ten, but I missed..."

Pause...

"Boss, I know. If you'll just let me..."

Pause...

"For fucks sake boss, the truck is in the dock. I missed the fuckin' boat!"

And he had. By about 30 feet. The thing that made my day was the fact that on board the truck was 20 tonnes of dried instant mashed potato in 1 tonne cardboard crates. It tickled me greatly to be able to record on my shipping documents "Departure delayed by 6 hours to allow the dredging of a mashed potato slick."

Back to the tale...I woke at 6 am. Woke is perhaps too enthusiastic a word. I drifted from a world of dreamt pain into a word of real pain. Behind my eyes a chorus-line of clog-wearing marmosets tap-danced to the rhythm of my none-too-regular heartbeat. Sometime during the night my mouth had been visited by an incontinent goat and somebody had fastened my bladder to an airline. Oh Gods! I made a note to throw out my watch, in favour of one with a quieter *TICK,* and tried to remember where the hell I was, and why. This in itself was a bad idea, because I suddenly remembered and sat up,

For any of you who are unaware of the physical organisation of your average articulated lorry cab, let me explain. Behind the seats is a bottom bunk bed. Usually made of old road surface and hard core, the bed is designed to fit anyone up to five feet eleven inches tall. I am six feet one. Above the bottom bunk is usually suspended another bunk bed, which is an ideal shelf for storing all those things that you really want to hit the windscreen at speed when you brake hard. The distance between top and bottom bunk is exactly five inches less than the room you take up when you sit up suddenly...

After the pain subsided I struggled free of the cab and went and hammered on Alan's cab door. The face that appeared at the window had exactly the expression I was sure my face wore. One of incredible suffering, confusion and a slowly waking realisation that we had screwed up royally. After morning ablutions, we went to the coffee shop, had three cups of strong black coffee and then decided we had to go. We were both sober. Painfully, nauseatingly sober, or I would not have even considered driving, no matter how urgent the load. Hangovers serve as a reminder that men are, on the whole, little boys who should know better...

We had to be in Bordeaux that same night. Needless to say, it didn't happen. We stopped at every service station on the way, to get coffee, to be ill, or to sleep. Eventually, at the end of the driving day we had made it as far as La Rochelle, which was, at least, within shouting distance of Bordeaux. And Alan produced a bottle of wine. We looked at it, then threw it in the bin, and made coffee.

I eventually got to Alicante just a day late and by great good fortune this was not a problem, as the factory was not actually expecting the delivery at a set time. I located the factory, after several false starts and diversions, but I felt like death warmed up. My head was really pounding. The office was on the second floor and I took the paperwork to the young lady at the front desk. I must have looked like hell, because she asked if I was okay. After I explained that I had a really bad head she reached into her desk and produced a glass vial, which she broke open and poured the contents into a beaker, which was in turn topped up with water from the water cooler.

"Drink that!" she commanded.

It was very bitter, but I was dehydrated and would have drunk it had it been lemon juice. Within a matter of two minutes my head no longer hurt. I asked her what it was.

"Morphine," she grinned.

Needless to say, the rest of the day went well and in a blur. I could happily have unloaded the sheepskins by hand and probably faster than the forklift that actually did the job. Wheeee!

Trailer unloaded, I phoned my boss, who had organised a reload of oranges from Valencia, at the fruit market. The load was organised by an old friend, Enrique, and was not to be collected until Monday of the following week. This meant I would have to entertain myself for five days, in spring, in Valencia. What a dreadful thing to happen!

The fruit market was about a quarter of a mile from the beach, so I dropped the trailer in the trailer park and took the unit to the sea front, where it is possible to park within fifty feet of the ocean. Just to make the thing perfect, the Dutchman's bar was two hundred yards away, a good restaurant owned by an English lass and her husband was within walking distance, and there was a canned drink dispenser actually on the beach, within ten feet of where I parked. And this machine vended ice-cold lager. Sometimes life could be good.

Five days later, I made my way to the Valencia fruit market. Enrique, it has to be said, was not happy. Apparently he had to bribe the stevedores to load my trailer, due to the dreadful smell that lingered on the sheets and timbers. However, true to his word, he had got the trailer loaded and the paperwork was in order, so I had a look round the load, made sure it was secure, and coupled up the wagon. All was not well, however, as I noticed when I came to the first big hill. The truck did not want to pull, and before long I was being overtaken by pedal cyclists, and on one occasion a smug looking tortoise. It became painfully obvious that the fuel filter was blocking up and as a result I was laying down a smoke screen worthy of James Bond. I felt that I had been here before. Indeed I had…and I had used my last spare fuel filter…

Mr Boss, when I phoned him, was not impressed. Nor was he prepared to pay out for a breakdown company to come to my aid. His only advice was, "Get the bloody thing back before Thursday, or make sure it is parked up, and empty when you get back, 'cos you won't have a job!" Or words to that effect. It was a shame Martin was not in the office, rather than his partner, as I was more likely to get helpful advice from him. Oh well.

I removed the fuel filter, and washed it through. This was briefly effective, but after 100 or so miles the same problem occurred. Wash, rinse and repeat all the way to the French Spanish border. Which is why I found myself under a Spanish truck in the early hours of the morning, very quietly swapping fuel filters. If, by chance, you were the person who suddenly discovered his truck was lacking *OOMPH* one spring morning, then all I can do is apologise, but I was working for a tyrant, and I was a lot further away from home than you were…

Tired truck

When you drive trucks for a living it is inevitable that not only will you witness more accidents than other people, you will eventually have one. The thing is, when you drive a thirty eight tonne truck the accidents are likely to be more epic than usual...

When it became obvious that the company I was working for was in serious trouble financially (and you can tell this when your pay cheque bounces for the third time in seven weeks) I decided to bail out, and quit.

That left me with a bit of a problem, in that I had no job to go to, but I decided to ring one of the directors of the company we had been sub-contracting for. I'd first met Bob when he was going to Cherbourg on the same Truckline Ferry as I was. He was a lovely man with a love of the whole business of transport and a genuine interest in his drivers. So I was not surprised, when I rang him, for him to know exactly who I was, who I worked for, and the problems we were having.

"I don't suppose you have any jobs going? I really am desperate," I pleaded.

"If you can be here in forty five minutes, you're on!" he replied. And I was. However, he neglected to mention the work I would be doing was what we called 'Tramping,' which was basically driving round the UK all week, and sleeping in the truck, so I had no clothing, no food, no money, no bedding...it was a long week.

I went home on the Friday night and he rang me on the Saturday morning, and asked if I would be prepared to do night 'trunking' from the Lichfield depot to Poole. This seemed like a good plan, and I agreed. It was decided that for now I would be a 'temp' and we'd see how things went. In fact this arrangement continued for about six months, during which time I did a lot of Poole work, a few continental trips, in fact anything they asked. It was fun, educational and legal, which was a novelty for me. And the wages were far and away better than I had with my previous employer.

Then, one night...

I'd collected a pre-loaded trailer from the Lichfield depot, for delivery to the Olympic Village which was being constructed in Barcelona. My job, of course, was to take it to the docks for shipping abroad. When I looked at it, the load consisted of sheets of concrete reinforcement wire mesh, stacked almost to the ceiling of the curtain-sided trailer. I was not too happy with the way it had been secured to the trailer, so I had a word with the chaps in the warehouse. He let me take a half dozen ratchet straps and I secured the load to my specifications, re-sheeted it and set off.

Within about a mile I was beginning to think something was not quite right. I couldn't really describe it, but there was a certain feel about the way the rig was handling, a certain 'looseness' round corners. I stopped, checked the fifth wheel, the tyres and the load security, and in spite of my reservations all seemed well, so I set off again.

Once I reached the A38 the truck seemed to have settled down, although in truth there was very little on that road to unsettle it, being a series of mild undulations and curves with no real geographic features. Until, that is, you approached one particular roundabout, where the road has a series of sweeping bends, left, right, left, then the roundabout itself, then a further quick left, right left combination off the roundabout exit.

As I turned off the roundabout to continue up the A38 I felt a jolt from the trailer, as if it had been rammed from the rear. At the same time I had to follow the road curve to the right, and again the *kick* and this time immediately followed by a sickening lurch, and all of a sudden the truck and trailer were on their side, and I was suddenly sat nine feet in the air, and parallel to the ground.

This is not an ideal place to be. Fortunately I was wearing my seatbelt and so was not thrown around the cab. Unfortunately I was a bit disorientated and undid that same seatbelt, before I realised that it was the only thing keeping gravity at bay…

As I picked myself out of the broken glass I discovered several things.

Firstly, denim does not protect against glass shards. I had just fallen nine feet onto the result of the wing mirror going through the side window, but my fall had been broken by my buttocks.

Secondly, when the cab is orientated as it should be, it is a wonderful, homely environment. However, if you rotate that environment ninety degrees it is suddenly very hostile indeed.

Thirdly, you tend to not be thinking too clearly after a shock like that. People yelling at you to 'Get out before it explodes!' have been watching too many American dramas. Diesel is not highly explosive under normal circumstances. It is not liable to explode as soon as you have a shunt. However, when the brain is rattled, you tend to ignore this and react to the fear, rather than the logic.

Fourthly, all the broken glass at your feet may indicate that the windscreen is smashed. However, it is possibly an idea to test this theory by trying to touch it, rather than smashing against it with your nose in your attempt to get out through an intact Triplex laminated glass windscreen.

Fifthly, cross-cab access on a Daf 95 series truck is brilliant, when it is the right way up. When all fallen over, you discover you have to climb nine feet into the air to get to the driver's door.

Sixthly, the nice driver's door, that closes with such a satisfying **CLUNK** when you shut it, weighs a bloody tonne when you have to push it up into the air with one hand, whilst holding on to the seat with your other.

Seventhly, once you are finally through the door, the electric windows are large enough to pass your body through, as you find out when you absently step back...

And eighthly, when you do finally get out of the cab and are standing, surrounded by people, nine feet in the air, it is a hell of a long way to get down..

A kindly stranger allowed me to ring the Lichfield depot and explain the problem. As it happened, the problem was greater than I imagined, as the A38 had to be shut, and traffic from Lichfield in one direction, Drayton Manor in another and Minworth in a third, was all backed up for miles. Apparently it made the Radio One traffic report, but I missed this as I was busy panicking.

I surveyed the scene. The tractor unit was on its side entirely, but the trailer was leaning crazily against a partially flattened street lighting pole. Oh boy...there goes my job.

Bob's son, who was a transport officer in the company, turned up, and parked his MR2 beside the truck. He was unhappy and started to have a go at me. I felt too confused to really reply. I'd had a bang on the head, and several cuts and scrapes in the incident. Then Bob turned up, and typically for him, his only concern was that I was okay. The truck, he reasoned, was insured. These things happen, and he was fairly certain they'd find out why it happened. Although, he cautioned, if I was found to have been speeding, then I would certainly be out of a job. In this I knew I was safe. I do not break speed limits knowingly, even now, so I was happy with that codicil.

Bob arranged for me to go with him back to the depot, then get a lift home and if I was up to it I could come back in the morning to fill in the insurance details. As we headed for his Mercedes, there was a yell, a squeal, and the lamp-post gave way. The trailer ended up entirely on its side, but the lamp post landed fairly and squarely across the roof of the MR2...

Next day I wandered in to the yard and Bob and his co-director Steve came to see me. After I'd filled in the insurance details Steve told me he was rather happy to say that the police had taken all the tacho discs of mine from the truck, and as far as they could tell there was not one single infraction on any of them. They had told Steve they were considering prosecuting me for an insecure load originally, as they were of the opinion that the load had shifted and thrown the centre of balance out. However, a Transport Ministry representative at the scene pointed out to them that even with the trailer on its side the load was still entirely unmoved. Apparently it had taken three hours to unload the trailer prior to righting it, so securely was it fastened.

I was pleased about this, but irked that I would probably not have a job by the end of the day. After all, I had been at least partially responsible for folding the son of the boss' MR2 nearly in half. Even this, it seemed, was not a problem. The car was a company car, leaked like a sieve, and would now be replaced by the insurance.

Bob looked up at me.

"Oh yeah. One more thing. Because of this, I suppose you realise, as of today you can no longer be a temp?"

I sighed. I'd expected this, but it still hurt. I liked the job, I liked the company and I liked the people I worked with. Oh well, back to the agencies.

I nodded, and went to stand up. Bob looked at Steve, who burst out laughing.

"Yeah, as of nine o'clock this morning, you're a fully employed driver. How do you fancy Spain, like you did with your old boss?"

Like? LIKE? I have to say my exit was not the most dignified. I danced round the yard grinning like a loon!

Post Script:

The reason the truck fell over was eventually discovered partly by maths, and partly by luck. We had a number of similar incidents, and finally the company engineer got together with the trailer manufacturer. It was discovered that certain loads which were not excessively heavy but carried their mass high in the trailer, would, when coupled to certain tractor units with a steering middle axle, become horribly unstable at over 30 mph. The solution was bizarrely simple. The rear axle of the trailer was moved back six inches on all of the trailers of this type, and the problem went away. It was not my fault at all. Geometry did it!

Olympic Torched

So, finally I was settled into a good job with a company that did not encourage lawlessness, that had the financial backing to pay wages regularly and that actually cared about the welfare of its staff. What on earth could go wrong? Take one step forward, Mr Murphy...

The first job I had with the company after rolling their truck was to take the load that was on the fateful trailer down to the Olympic Village in Barcelona. The load had been transferred onto another, rather older trailer and was waiting for me when I entered the yard, three days later. Much to my embarrassment there were a number of my work mates standing by the gate as I drove in, and they all cheered, jeered and blew raspberries as I arrived.

Once again I made sure the load was secure and that the trailer was up to the job. The load was a trailer full of steel reinforcing mesh for concrete and whilst it did not weigh a great deal it filled the trailer from floor to roof, front to back. Whilst checking the straps that held it securely to the trailer I noted that there was a very large tear in the canvas of the roof, which was most certainly not waterproof and was at a stage where it was shredding into ribbons and streamers.

I pointed this out to the office, who decided that I should press on, and they would make arrangements for the trailer to receive attention either before or after I unloaded at the Olympic Village complex in Barcelona.

I loaded my bag of clothing, briefcase full of maps, my box of tinned food, my fridge of drinks and fresh food, and all the other paraphernalia that makes a truck driver's life easier, then I set out down the road. I will confess that my main concern was to check that the darned trailer was not going to lie down on the job. To my great relief it stuck to the road and handled faultlessly and so I set off to Poole and the Truckline ferry Coutance, which would whisk me in opulent luxury to the port of Cherbourg. Okay, I lied about the luxury, but there would at least be a bed and a shower.

Having disembarked at Cherbourg, and cleared customs (for this is the time before the border controls were lifted, and each county had its own routines for slowing your entry to a crawl) I drove down the road to the company's Cherbourg office and made myself known there. Jean Paul was in the office and greeted me with the traditional French remark

"Hi! Wanna coffee?"

Coffee. The bane of my life and yet at the same time the very lifeblood that courses through my veins. If you do not want an addiction do not work in France. Do not go on holiday in France. Do not visit France. Do not, if you can help it even read the word France. Every service station in France has a coffee vending machine and not just an instant coffee-like warm drink-serving machine. These machines grind the beans, pass hot water over them and serve the wonderfully aroma'd, golden brown coloured elixir in a horrible brown plastic cup. By the end of the first year of working abroad I was drinking 40 plus cups of coffee a day. I got to the stage where I needed two cups of coffee in the morning just to jump-start my heart. Over the years I have cut back, first by diluting the life-giving fluids with milk and sugar, and finally by main force. I am now, as my friends will attest, down to between fifteen and twenty cups a day. As I sit here I can hear Mr Blup-Blup, my Percolating God, as if boils, hisses and steams its way to producing another two litres of coffee. I am a lost cause. Do not, if you can help it, go the way I did. But yet again I digress...

Having sorted out with Jean-Paul exactly where I was going, and when I needed to be there, I re-iterated my concerns about the roof of the trailer. Jean-Paul rang Pascal, our agent in Barcelona, and asked him to make arrangements for the trailer to be repaired when I got there. Thus assured, I set off to Barcelona.

By the time I got to the first night's rest stop in Bordeaux the tear had become a series of streamers, each about six feet long, flapping and whipping about in the breeze. To be honest it was more distracting than dangerous, but to try and reduce the problem I threw a couple of straps over the roof and ratcheted them down tightly. This seemed to help somewhat, in that when I carried on the next day it didn't appear that I had a trailer full of incredibly tall drum majorettes.

La Jonquera, gateway to Spain, on the Mediterranean coast, and accessed via the 'Viaduc De Pox,' the butt of many a childish truck driver's jokes. I pulled in to the TIR park, located the agent's office and presented myself and my paperwork to her. She handed me a note in return, from Pascal, instructing me to go directly to Vic, and there get the canvas sealed and welded. From there I was to go directly to the Olympic Village and unload.

A brief stop at the restaurant on the main road for the inevitable cup of coffee, then off I set. I like the main road from La Jonquera to Barcelona. It seems to encapsulate the spirit of Spain, the very essence of the lifestyle. Houses, mere frameworks of bricks, were being lived in whilst they were being built. Vineyards and olive groves to right and left, old tractors driven by older farmers as they ploughed tiny strips of land. Then suddenly, with no warning a massive industrial estate, festooned with advertising billboards, lit with neon and arc lights, and then just as suddenly back to the nature-dictated pace of the countryside. I loved it.

And then you I got to Gerona. Oh my word. To the left, by the peage, there was a red and white striped chimney and beyond that the paper mill of Torras Papel. The views were wonderful, but the smell from the adjoining papermill was quite literally stunning. It has been too many years since I last drove that route, but I think even now, were you to blindfold me and drive me down the road I could still tell you when we were within ten yards of the chimney…

The town of Vic was divided by time in the same way as so much of Spain. Both ancient and modern, tranquil and busy, industrial and agricultural. I can think of no place in the UK that has such a fusion of two eras. The past, now retired and relaxed, watching through half closed eyes as the present becomes the thrusting, energetic, exciting future. Two polar opposites, existing in harmony, and between them generating an excitement for what tomorrow may bring.

I pulled into a warehouse at the address I had been given, and an elderly man with the most incredible moustache came out to greet me. I tried so very hard to look him in the eye as I spoke, but my gaze was drawn inevitably back to the waxen ends of the facial hair. At every movement of his face they moved. When he spoke the left hand end seemed to be trying to conduct the Minute Waltz, whilst the right one described lazy figure of eights in the air.

Eventually I gave up and just handed him the note. He read it and the moustache nodded in agreement, as he pointed that I should take my truck into the shed.

Inside the building a young lad was eating his lunch, but put it down when summoned by the Moustache. I was introduced as 'Senór Ingles,' and immediately the lad became as animated as the end of the 'tache. In an interesting patois of Spanish and English he explained that he spoke the "English good," as his mother was brought up in Scotland. His excited chattering was quite endearing, and would have been more so had his lunch not apparently consisted of raw onion and blue cheese, and had he not deemed it important to be bilingual in quite such close proximity. However, I have to say that to this day I have never heard an accent so incredibly tortuous as that of an English speaking Scots Spaniard.

After a while The Moustache was able to calm him to such an extent that he could actually start work on the trailer repair. The canvas of the trailer is actually a material coated in a rubbery plastic. These days it is not unknown for the fabric to be interwoven with wires, which not only re-enforce the material but can also be combined with an anti theft circuit to make it less likely for the canvas to be cut and the contents pilfered. On mine, however, it was just the standard rubber-coated cloth, and as such repaired by a combination of a petroleum-based adhesive and a hot air welding gun.

This, of course, was the point at which it all went wrong. The youth sat up to ask me a question, and knocked over the pot of adhesive. He had the presence of mind to turn off the hot air gun and tried to tidy up the glue that was oozing over the newly repaired surface. Unfortunately the consistency of the spillage was such that it did not lend itself to being recovered, so the lad instead busied himself by trying to wipe it up with huge swathes of blue paper towels. This was no more successful than the attempts at recovery, but at least spread the substance thinly over about two square meters of the roof, although it meant that I now had a trailer with a roof consisting at least partly of rubberised tissue paper.

As soon as the lad has climbed down off the trailer I moved the whole rig outside, because to be honest the smell of the solvent was beginning to melt the wax in my ears. I thanked the two ends of the moustache, its owner and the youth, and set off for the Olympic Village.

I arrived at the building site at exactly the wrong time. The site was at lunch and all was quiet. The site foreman directed me, with much pointing of his bottle of San Miguel, to park the trailer under the huge tower crane that was servicing the builders. To my left was the hotel being built by an English company and to my right the Spanish equivalent. They looked magnificent, although as I glanced up at the builders, casually sitting on jutting girders several hundred feet in the air my toes did try to gain extra purchase on the dusty site under my feet.

So entranced was I at the antics of these human flies that at first I did not register the shouting behind me. It was not until the site foreman grabbed my shoulder that I looked away from the construction. I followed his gaze.

My trailer, so recently repaired, was on fire. Sheets of flame and sooty, oily black smoke boiled off the roof. In seconds the whole of the roof was ablaze. I was briefly stunned at the speed of the conflagration, but realised I needed to do something fast. I jumped up on the catwalk between the trailer and truck unit and turned off the isolator valves on the airlines, then jumped down and as the trailer rained burning plastic around me I pulled the fifth wheel release lever, and dived into the cab.

It was not the most sedate start I have ever made in a truck. The cabin shook as I dropped the clutch and the truck broke free of the trailer. I hadn't bothered undoing the airlines, nor had I dropped the legs on the trailer, so as the trailer fell off the end of the truck it simultaneously ripped the wiring cables and airlines out of the back. However, having isolated the lines at the valves, I was able to drive off without the air escaping.

As I was driving the unit to safety a red Unimog 4 wheel drive fire truck came the other way. Three firemen attacked the blaze, but in the short time it had taken, the sheeting was almost completely devoured and the supporting wooden structure beyond repair.

This was not good. In the space of less than a week I had managed to write off two trailers and one truck, whilst delivering the same load! Lets face it, I was screwed. I'd be lucky if the company would even pay my fare home!

I stood by my truck, looking at the conflagration and feeling a sense of desperation. I so badly wanted this job. I loved the work and loved the company I worked for. Yet I could see no way of surviving this disaster. A hand grabbed my shoulder.

"Hi, I'm Pascal. I'm the Company agent for Barcelona. That looked nasty. I tell you what, it could have cost us a fortune if you hadn't dragged the truck out of there. I don't know whether you were brave or stupid, putting yourself at risk to save the company property like that!"

At this point I very nearly told him the only reason I moved the truck was because it had all my possessions in it, including my passport and wallet. However, something made me shut up and nod sagely. Suddenly I had a feeling things were going to work out okay after all…

Pulling Rank

Of course, it isn't just Murphy and nature that can conspire to totally screw up your day. Sometimes you can't help but wonder whether the people surrounding you are part of a monstrous practical joke. Some days you just know you should have stayed in bed. This, I decided, was one of them…

I had loaded some office furniture from a factory in Strasbourg, an event that had in itself been, if not eventful, then at least indicative of the direction the whole journey back was going to take.

I had never been to this factory before, nor indeed to Strasbourg, but I was vastly impressed by the scenery on the route from the Citroen factory in Metz through the mountains. On the way I had encountered a thunderstorm of biblical proportions and rain that made me seek a convenient lay-by. When you can barely see the road in front of you, you know it is time for a break. As I entered the city I was awed by the vast number of rail-tracks on the right and agog at the TGV train set on a concrete plinth to the left hand side of the motorway. Here, clearly, was the hub of the French train industry.

The factory was located behind a housing estate, easily navigated, and I pulled in to the front gates just as the sun was setting. I asked the gatehouse operator where I should go and he replied "Le Porte Verte." I was slightly concerned, as I was not sure whether he had said "The green door" (Le porte verte) or "The glass door" (Le porte de verre), but I would be able find out when I went round the corner.

As I pulled in, a truck came the other way. I flashed him through and he flashed me, so I moved, and so did he. I stopped, and he stopped. I flashed him again, and he flashed me.

I moved, he moved. At this point I realised I was actually seeing my own reflection in a huge glass window of an office block in the twilight…

I turned the corner, looking for either a glass door or a green door. In front of me was a green door. Right beside it was a glass one… I chose the green door, and went in, and discovered that both doors opened in to the same office. I located the person in charge of the loading, and was told that the job was "drop and swap," that is, I dropped my empty trailer and collected a full one. Easy!

Having swapped trailers, I decided that rather than press on I would spend the night in the factory yard and set out at about 6am the following morning. After a quick shower in the factory washrooms, I cooked myself a meal in café camion and settled down for the night. What could be simpler?

OOMPAH OOMPAH BOOM BOOM!

My immediate reaction was to reach for the snooze button. Except I couldn't find one. Real life does not, sadly, come with a snooze system. I glanced at the clock on the dashboard. 10:30pm local time. What in the name of all that is holy was happening?

Investigation proved that my idea of parking the truck against the compound fence was not one of my better decisions. The tavern bar on the other side of the fence apparently hosted live local talent, and being on the French/German border, there was a certain Germanic influence on tonight's star turn, a large band of tubas, accordions, drums and singers. Oh well, they couldn't keep this up for long, could they? Actually, by 12:30am I was beginning to wonder if A) they could actually keep it up forever, and B) if that really only knew three tunes! Finally, however, peace prevailed, and I slept until the alarm clock went off at 5:30am.

The trip back went fairly smoothly from there. I had been allocated a Zeebrugge to Felixstowe crossing, which suited me, as it shaved about an hour off the travelling time to the dock, and I arrived with a couple of hours to spare before the boat was due. I had time to snatch a coffee at the café in the port office and watch as the P&O Ferry berthed. It occurred to me that apart from my truck and two others, all the rest of the vehicles waiting to cross were military vehicles. I can remember thinking at the time that having the military on board should make for a quiet crossing and quick exit at Felixstowe. Events would prove me wrong…

The usual routine on disembarking at Felixstowe was to drive from the boat through the Customs shed, where if the Customs officers were interested they would pull you on to a bay. It was, occasionally, inconvenient, but rules are rules. On this occasion I found myself behind an army Landrover. A Customs Official wandered over and started chatting with the passenger, an impressive looking officer with lots of braid, and a huge handlebar moustache. There seemed to be a bit of informal banter and then things seemed to get a bit tense, so, being nosy, I got out to check my oil and listen in to the conversation, which went something like this…

Customs Officer: "I need to see what is in that locked box."

Army Officer: "I am sorry, but I can't show you. It is covered by the official secrets act and you may not look inside without authorisation."

CO: "Look, I am simply trying to do my job. I will not allow you to enter this country unless I see inside that box."

AO: "Fine, I'm sure we have sufficient stores to stay here for a couple of weeks at least. But you are not seeing inside that box without proper authorisation."

CO: "Your men can go. They've been cleared. But I will see inside that box, before you leave here!"

AO: "If I stay, they stay. And no, you won't."

At this stage the Customs Officer got on his radio and within two or three minutes there were maybe ten Customs Officials surrounding the Landrover.

CO: "You will now show me what is in the box!"

AO: "Is it my turn?"

He too got on the radio and within 30 seconds there were somewhere in the region of sixty heavily armed soldiers surrounding the Customs Officers.

AO: "Your move…"

The Customs Officer, at this point, decided that he was not going to call the bluff of several dozen armed men, and let everyone through. As the Landrover passed him the Army officer nodded and saluted most politely. The Customs Officer was less formal in his mode of address.

I, of course, was in fits of laughter, a fact that did not escape the Customs Officer, which is why I spent the next 24 hours in a cell whilst my truck was painstakingly searched. Most unfair!

Uppers and Downers

Unless the writers are the Brothers Grimm, life seldom resembles a fairy story. In my experience it can go from farce to tedium to heart-stopping shock in a very short time.

There are occasions when a job starts to go wrong and the train of events becomes more and more derailed as the job continues. On these occasions all you can do is carry on and try and make the most of it. On this occasion the train not only left the tracks, it careered down a hill and fell in to a river, with me hanging on to the brakes and praying for the ride to end...

On the Thursday on which the job began, I had returned from a spectacularly disastrous week in Spain and France, and was looking forward to a few days at home. It had been a rush to get back to the UK, as my year-long passport had expired on Thursday and I needed to be in the UK to renew it. Besides which, I was owed a couple of days at home and had been promised that I would be allowed a long weekend.

Unfortunately for me a vital job had occurred, due to an error in the office and they asked me if I would please get an urgent load from Ford in Dagenham to Ford in Valencia. And it had to be there for Saturday morning. Therefore I had to rush, on foot, to a post office and renew my passport. The post office, when I arrived, had no photo booth, so at 5:15pm I could be seen running through an Essex town, trying to find a store with a photo booth. As a result my passport photo for the year portrayed me as an unkempt wild-eyed sweaty lump, red of face and staring of eye.

I returned to the post office just as they were closing and they kindly let me in and processed my passport. I'm not sure whether it was due to the milk of human kindness that runs through the veins of post office staff, or the fact they were terrified of the wild-eyed apparition that faced them, wheezing, panting and sweating at the door!

After that, it could only be plain sailing, surely? I pulled in to the factory which was expecting the tiles I had on board. They decided that rather than stripping the trailer, they would unload the tiles from the back door, which, incidentally, I had not used on the trip at all. I unlocked the catches, and swung the door open. It promptly fell off, on to my head.

The next thing I can remember clearly is being in our shipping office in Poole, with a blood-soaked bandage on my head. The officer in charge was a little concerned that I was zoned out and was of the opinion I should not ship out. I, on the other hand, was not really in any condition to make a decision and decided to carry on. I had tipped the load of tiles, driven to Ford, loaded and processed the paperwork and driven to Poole, and to this day I cannot remember much about it…

The journey itself is a blur. I can remember the headache, but little about the trip. However, I do remember driving through Madrid at about 2am, and being confronted by a police officer, who was stopping HGV vehicles for a roadside check. He waved me in to the lay-by. I can remember waving back…and driving on. And I got away with it!

I really can't say how many laws I broke on the way down to Valencia. I know that had I been compos mentis I would never have taken the risk, but head injuries tend to blur the line between sensible and stupid. Nevertheless I arrived at Almusaffes, just south of Valencia, at 8am on Saturday morning, and pulled in to the Ford factory just in time. Tipping was completed by 9:30am and I readied myself for a quiet weekend. I rang the Bournemouth office of my company, and told them I was empty. Unfortunately they had organised a reload, again for urgent delivery, so my weekend of peace and quiet on a sunny beach was ruined.

Valencia produces some fine porcelain, and my reload was three tonnes of some of their finest. From ornate birdbaths to intricately decorated wall tiles, floral vases to small silver and gold plated ornaments, all were carefully loaded onto the trailer by hand and I oversaw the roping down. Blankets and padding were placed between the boxed products and the freestanding pieces were wrapped in bubble wrap. To give you some idea of the value of the load, the manager gave me a small porcelain ornament as a thank you present for helping with the loading. It is an owl and three owlets on a branch, with gold leaf decoration and measured maybe three inches by an inch. The detail was incredible, and it was in their catalogue for just over £200, in 1988...

Customs clearance was arranged via an agency in La Jonquera, on the north Mediterranean coast of Spain and I decided it would probably be worth my while setting out to get there on the Saturday, as it would mean I had a secure parking area to keep the load safe.

At the time I was in a Mercedes truck, a nice reliable wagon with EPS electronic gearshift, making it a joy to drive. With the total weight of the load being under three tonnes, the drive back was going to be easy, so I decided to go over the mountain rather than follow the coast road. For the first forty-five minutes the journey was uneventful and as I went up the long, wide mountain road I passed a number of trucks and cars.

My first indication of trouble was when, on a flat section of road, my speed started to decrease. Vehicles that I had passed with ease on the incline were passing me on the flat. Before long I was impeding the passage of cyclists and pedestrians and so I pulled into a lay-by, co-incidentally opposite a bar. It was just midday. I phoned my company's mechanic in Lichfield, and he gave me the number of the Mercedes breakdown company in Valencia. They in turn said that they were busy, but would get someone to me as soon as possible. So I had a meal at the bar, and a cup of coffee, and waited.

It was just before midnight that a chap wandered in to the bar. He turned out to be the mechanic I was waiting for and I took him to see the truck. Having started the engine and listened for a while he declared that he could not repair it on site, but would have to tow it to the workshop. But with what? In answer, he wandered off, and returned a short while later in a Mercedes estate car, which he reversed up to the front of the truck. I wound down the legs of the trailer and uncoupled it, started the truck so I could pull the wagon from under the trailer, and then he produced a rigid tow bar from the rear of the car. Strewth! He was serious!

I was already somewhat concerned about the idea of being towed by a car and more so when he wound off the truck brakes. It made a sort of sense. With the engine dead I would not have air to operate the brakes and there was a danger they could lock on. However, one of the other problems with being engineless was the fact I'd have no power steering and manual steering on the Merc was darned heavy. It didn't help that I'd had little sleep and possibly more coffee than was good for me. And I was busting for a wee…I was concerned, but little knew that what was to follow would turn out to be possibly the second most scary 45 minutes of my entire life.

For the first few miles the journey was uneventful, and I began to relax. Then we encountered the hill. You may recall the hill I had to climb on the way to the breakdown? Well, now I had to do it downwards, attached to an estate car, whilst having no brakes and little in the way of steering. It quickly became a lot more interesting. The driver/mechanic was seated happily puffing on a cigar, one arm casually resting on the door. I, on the other hand, was tramping uselessly on non existent brakes and heaving on the steering wheel, all the time well aware that my bladder was unhappy with what was happening. Corners became real challenges, and as we descended the mountain, our speed increased. 50 MPH. 55. 60. 65! Oh my good god, we are going to DIE!

And then, just when I thought it could get no worse, my evil mind went **PING**!. Remember that village? Torres Torres? The one we go through every time we come up here?

The one with the narrow roads? The one with the really narrow single lane through the really twisty S bend? The one you struggle to get a truck through at 10 MPH? Well, guess what is waiting for you about 5 miles ahead? "

Oh Gods. I AM going to die!

A short while later a sign flashed past my peripheral vision. I only caught sight of it briefly, for I barely dare take my eyes off the road. It said 'Torres Torres.' I may have imagined it, but I am sure it had the words 'Welcome to your doom' in red letters underneath.

Fifty five miles an hour. That is the speed we went through the sinuous single carriageway road. I do not know how we got through it. By that time I was barely able to move my arms. The steering was so heavy that I was numb from my shoulders to my finger tips. My mouth was so dry I could feel the saliva crystallising on my tongue. I was not sweating. There was not sufficient moisture in my body to produce so much as a drop. All the moisture was collected in my bladder.

And we survived. We missed meeting anything coming the other way. I managed to turn the truck so that I didn't end up ruining some Spanish gentleman's siesta by parking a V8 diesel truck in his living room. No cyclists were harmed. I almost relaxed, but thought better of it. My bladder was in far too perilous a condition to allow for any muscle relaxation.

We arrived at the Mercedes dealer in Valencia. We stopped, the mechanic opened the twin metal gates and pulled the truck into the compound. He drove us round the showroom, past what turned out to be a hotel and restaurant complex, and to the back of the huge complex, to a parking bay for HGV vehicles. Then he did something I should possibly have paid more attention to, but I was, at that time, more concentrating on the fact that A) I was alive, and B) My bladder was seconds away from exploding. He stopped the vehicles, then, with the engine still running, he leapt out of the car, opened the boot, whipped the tow bar off in a rush, dumped it in the boot, ran back to the car, dived in and slammed the door. I remembered later that he had closed his window. Then he drove off, waving…

Oh well, given that I seemed to be alone, in a deserted truck park, I could have a wee. I opened the door and clambered out, and oh, the relief! I stood hosing down the front wheel for a couple of seconds when suddenly I heard a noise. Well, I say 'noise', but it was almost a sub audible rumbling. A vibration of the air. It was also something primal. Hair that I didn't have on the back of my neck tried to stand up. I lost all thoughts of weeing. And indeed the ability. I very carefully, very quietly, turned my head to see where the sub-harmonic thunder was coming from.

To this day I could not identify the breed. Imagine, if you will, Cerberus had had a bi-cranial amputation and taken to wearing a bearskin coat. Imagine he had decided that mustard yellow contact lenses were the latest fashion statement and had accessorised with strings of drool. That is what it was. And worse, there were three of it…

As luck would have it, I had left the cab door open in my haste to relieve myself and faster than I could think I was back in the doorway. The damned dogs, however, were faster, and one of them actually tore the seat right out of my jeans. But I was lucky. Half a second later he would be enjoying Buttock of Hunter Avec Levis…

So, there we were. Me, inside the cab, and those three devil hounds sat, waiting for me to do something interesting. And I did…I peed on them from the driver's door window. Well, I was busting, and their intervention had done nothing for my bladder control.

They were still there when I awoke later on the Sunday morning. And in the afternoon. The evening saw them lying, staring at the cab door, occasionally growling if they saw a movement. I was not too unhappy, as I had food and drink in the cab, and I was happy to pee on them whenever the need took me. However, there was one basic human need that would have to be dealt with before too long…Sunday night, and there they were, unmoved, just waiting for their nice foreign made chew-toy to leave the tin can it was delivered in.

Fortunately Monday happened, and when I woke the complex was humming in to life, and of the dogs there was no sign, apart from bits of concrete they had absentmindedly chewed on, and the odd truck back axle they had used as toothpicks.

After an urgent visit to the facilities in the dealership I found someone who could perhaps deal with the breakdown. The problems I faced then were getting authorisation to get the repair done, arranging for the valuable load to be collected and getting me back home. My office said they would arrange something to make sure I was home quickly, as they appreciated the urgent delivery, and they owed me a favour. And like a fool I believed them! My new bosses were more reliable than Mr Boss, but on occasions even they were not averse to stretching the truth if it meant that it got them out of a hole. The arrangements were made to divert a driver from Spain. He would drop his trailer at the Mercedes dealers, and then we would go and collect the trailer I had dropped and bring it back. The truck would be loaded on the trailer and we would take it to the docks, ship it back to the UK, and to the workshop in Bournemouth for repair. The best laid plans…

My colleague arrived at about mid-day. He was a tall grey-haired rubicund French chap and his first action when he arrived was to head for the bar café and buy a bottle of wine, which he drank, in its entirety. He followed it with a light meal, another bottle of wine and two beers. It would be safe to say that when we left the Mercedes complex he was somewhat the worse for wear...we weaved down the road, with him singing to himself and occasionally trying to enter in to conversation. Now, whilst I speak reasonably good French, his slurred and convoluted speech patterns made it virtually impossible to understand him, and after a short while we lapsed into companionable silence.

The journey back to the trailer was almost as nerve wracking as the trip to the dealership. As I already related, I loathe drunk drivers. Yet I needed transport. I badly wanted to get home. I'm ashamed to admit I allowed myself to be convinced he was under the limit. I really did want, and need, to get home. And yet my chauffer seemed to think he was driving a go-kart in a race, rather than an artic tractor unit. We left most of the corners travelling at least slightly sideways and came close to having a number of accidents. It was certainly an eye opener! By great good fortune we got to the trailer without actually suffering an accident, and at this point it all started to go even more wrong.

The truck phone rang. It was my boss in Bournemouth, who told me there had been a further change of plans. We were to deliver the load on the trailer, collect a reload, and then I was to be dropped at our Bordeaux depot, from whence to be taken to Cherbourg docks, and then over to the UK. Of course, as far as I was concerned, a major problem with that was that all my worldly goods, such as wallet, clothing, etc were all in the cab back in Valencia. Nonetheless I was told that the instructions still stood. My goods and chattels would be returned when the truck reached the UK.

Whilst I was talking on the phone my colleague coupled up the trailer, and by the end of the conversation we were ready to leave. He hopped in to the cab, pulled off, and *CRASH,* the trailer fell off! In his drunken state he'd forgotten to actually check the trailer was coupled. I got out to have a look. The trailer was on the deck and the airbrake lines were stretched to full length. As he'd raised the trailer support legs, it meant that to get it back sufficiently high to be able to couple it up, it would have to be wound back on the jacks, by hand. He handed me the jack handle, hopefully. I grinned, and handed it back. You did the job, you put it right, old son!

Whilst he struggled to wind the trailer up, I opened the back doors of the trailer. You remember I told you how well the porcelain had been packed? As soon as I opened the door it became clear that it was not packed anywhere near well enough to withstand such an impact. The ornate birdbath was now a vast three-dimensional jigsaw puzzle. The beautiful wall tiles were now porcelain crazy paving, and the vases were, at best, hardcore. I was so glad it wouldn't be up to me to explain this at the point of delivery!

Shaking my head, I closed the back door. The trailer was now at the correct height for connecting to the tractor unit and this time I made sure that the fifth wheel coupling was secure. And off we went, again…My colleague seemed to be recovering his faculties and we managed to make the border with no real incident, apart from witnessing two loonies in a Spanish registered Austin Allegro, with 20+ bales of hay tied to the roof.

After clearing customs we wandered through the Pyrenees and northwards. By this time it was getting late, and so we pulled in to a service station for the night. Here the problems continued. My wallet was in the truck in Spain, and I was hungry. I explained to my colleague, who shrugged, ordered a huge meal and ate it in front of me. He followed this up with a beer, but, bless him; he bought me a bottle of water!

Next…sleeping arrangements. I was allotted the top bunk. There were no pillows, and no bedding. My colleague had the bottom bunk, with two pillows and a thick sleeping bag. So thick, in fact, that he had to open he window to keep cool. On the top bunk I froze. No sleep happened that night and I was cold, tired, hungry and miserable. This was not my most favourite day.

The night dragged, long, cold and uncomfortable, and at 6am, when the service station opened, I crawled out of the truck and in to the relative warmth of the shop. The chap behind the counter asked if there was anything I wanted. I told him the whole story and bless him; he got me a coffee and croissant. Colleague surfaced at about seven, came in to the shop, and bought and consumed a huge breakfast. It occurred to me I had no washing materials either, so I was now cold, hungry, tired, uncomfortable and unkempt. What else could go wrong? Silly question, really…

We arrived at the delivery location, and a number of people came out to help unload. The look of horror on their faces was a picture. Devastation writ across each visage. The birdbath was apparently a special order for a special customer and the tiles had been on order for weeks. My colleague, who I had come to think of as a royal pain in the posterior, tried to tell them that the load was like that when he collected it. He was, it seems, unaware that I spoke good French, and was surprised when I put the customers straight in fairly forthright terms. This did our friendship no good at all. I helped with the unloading and the cataloguing of the devastation. For all the padding at least thirty percent of the goods were broken. The customer spoke to my boss and I was summoned to the phone. To say my boss was unhappy would be a massive understatement. It seems that my colleague had phoned his depot in France whilst I was in the shop and told them it was I who dropped the trailer.

I was lucky. On occasions in the past I had made errors, and on each occasion I had phoned my boss and told him, truthfully, of my cock-ups. As a result he was quite prepared to believe that I was telling the truth. He also promised me to have a word with the Bordeaux office to put them in the picture too.

Unloading complete, we headed to Pau, and a small Citroen storage depot, for a reload, and from there to the Bordeaux office. I'd not been in the office more than thirty seconds before I was summoned to see Jean-Paul, the manager there. Again, luck was with me. When I was working for my previous, now bankrupt, employer, I did three years worth of sub-contract work from the Cherbourg depot, and Jean-Paul was the manager there at the time. We knew each other well and had been out together on weekends when I was stuck in Cherbourg. He too knew of my reputation for honesty and was prepared to accept my explanation of what had happened. After I left my colleague was summoned. The interview was short, and when he left the office he was cursing and yelling at me in a very colourful French patois. It seems that this was not the first time he had been involved in drink-related incidents, but it would be his last for the company. He had been fired...

The rest of the week consisted of me being shuttled hither and thither, from depot to depot, truck to truck, until finally, unkempt, smelly, tired and massively fed up, I got in to Poole Docks at 6 am on Friday morning. I was without cash, clothes or mobile phone, which were on my truck, and which, incidentally, had arrived back at the depot some two days before I did. It was by the merest good fortune that I had my passport with me, or I would possibly still be waiting at the dock even now. But I was home. I was back in the UK. I wandered in to the office, wondering what else could go wrong. I'd been there no more than two minutes before Annette called me over for a phone call. It was my Girlfriend du jour.

"I'm so sorry...your Dad died this morning..."

Voulez vous couchet?

For all my protestations I have to admit that I have had more than my fair share of the bizarre, the comic and the downright weird. I'm not entirely sure whether this is simply due to me being drawn towards the absurd or whether I was dropped on my head as a baby and therefore see the world as a more entertaining place than it really is...

Once again I'd been promised an easy reload after 'going the extra mile' to get a load tipped. Once again I believed them. Once again I was going to be sorely disappointed. All I had to do was collect 20 pallets of roofing tiles from the outskirts of Barcelona. This should be a breeze. Unfortunately a breeze was one of the things that was missing...

The temperature, by the time I rolled into the factory, was over ninety degrees and promising to get hotter as the day progressed. Of course the load had to go in through the side of the trailer, which meant that the sheeting and boards had to come off. Before long I was down to shirt and shorts, and it soon became clear that white sheets in hot sun were a very bad idea...

By the time the trailer was ready I was ready to collapse. I made myself known to the young lady in the noticeably air-conditioned office and after organising a forklift to load the trailer, she led me to the factory floor. The factory was partly built into an ancient monastery, with the old stonework and architecture blending uncomfortably with the new technology. In one corner was a stone circle about 5 feet across, with a wooden lid. She opened the lid and suggested I pull on the rope tethered to the stonework. A few pulls on the rope revealed a large glass jar, full of ice cold water. The water was fresh and sweet, better by far than the water from taps or bottles, and had been bubbling through the rocks into the well for five hundred years or more. At that moment I would not have exchanged it for the most expensive champagne…

I stood and watched the forklift putting and popping as 20 pallets of red roofing tiles were loaded and then reversed the sheet stripping process. The action was hampered by the fact that the now exposed steelwork had been absorbing the sunlight for an hour, and was now too hot to touch with exposed skin. Consequently I had to wear a pair of overalls to re-sheet the trailer and I was exhausted by the time I'd rebuilt and re-sheeted. More water was procured and I took the liberty of filling a few glass bottles to keep in the truck with me.

Everything being secure, I obtained the paperwork, settled into the cab and rang the office to find out what was wanted. Naturally, there had been a change of plan and the easy job was about to get more complicated. I would have to go to Vic, and load some hazardous chemicals in the morning…

Vic is a nice place, and apart from two occasions I have always liked going there. The first was when I nearly removed my knee on broken glass, and the second was when I was nearly blown up by a terrorist

After a quiet night in a secluded industrial estate I was woken at 6am by industrious happy little noises. I surfaced and peered out. People were pootling about outside, doing the sort of things people do on industrial estates, and doing it industriously. After a coffee I went to find the office and organised 6 barrels of a fairly noxious oxidising agent to be loaded. I was imagining them to be 5 litre containers, so was somewhat surprised to have six 45 gallon drums loaded.

Having secured the load I took the truck to the weighbridge, got a weight ticket, showing 37.8 tonnes, sorted out the hazchem [2] paperwork, arranged the orange hazardous

---

[2]   The rules for carrying materials regarded as hazardous are comprehensive, strict and rigorously policed. You may have seen trucks and trailers bearing large orange

chemical reflective plates on the cab and trailer, and rang my office to tell them I was loaded. To my annoyance I was told I had to go and collect some paper from a paper factory in Gerona. I explained that I was just a fraction under 38 tonnes, which was the maximum allowed in the UK, but was assured that the paper was for delivery in France, and European maximum weight allowance was 40 tonnes. Easy reload? I think not!

The address I was given was not, I discovered, the Gerona factory, but one in St Joan Les Fonts. I'd never been to this factory, but had heard of it, and the awkward loading bays. The factory was a redevelopment of a much older paper manufacturing plant and whilst over the years the equipment and processes had been upgraded and improved, the actual building infrastructure was from the age of horses and carts.

Off I footled, along the motorway to Gerona, then turned left, and began to climb. And climb. The map never shows just how steep the roads can get in the Pyrenees and this was steep! Before long the clouds above became the fog all around and still I climbed, until finally I emerged into brilliant sunshine, and a small village. The factory entrance was on the right and I pulled in. After visiting the office I was directed to a loading bay which had obviously been designed by someone with a sense of humour. It was required that you should reverse from bright sunlight into an unlit bay, barely wider than the trailer, itself a tricky prospect, but to complicate matters further someone had put an ornamental fountain in just

---

plates to front and rear. These are HAZCHEM markers, and inform the relevant authority that the vehicle is carrying a hazardous load. Other markings and stickers provide further information for the emergency services as required.

Although technically any goods carried in mainland Europe are transported under the ADR and Kemler regulations, the word HAZCHEM is generally used to convey the same meaning.

the right place to make a straight reverse impossible. The only advantage I had was that my truck was left hand drive and so at least I was on the right side to be able to see the entry in the mirrors properly. After a lot of cursing I managed to get the trailer on to the bay and opened the doors. This, I confidently expected, would be the worst loading bay I was ever likely to encounter. In retrospect, I should have realised that was a stupid thing to think.

Two pallets of paper later and I'm off to the Bordeaux depot.

On arrival, I popped in to the office to see Jean-Paul, the manager, who arranged for the hazardous portion of the load to be removed, and asked me if I'd mind 'just popping the pallets of paper to the delivery address.' Alarm bells failed to go off. Warning sirens noticeably failed to warn. I happily agreed to deliver them. After all the delivery address was just down the road. What could go wrong?

The first sign of an answer to the question was when I was flagged down by a gendarme, about an hour in to the trip. He wanted to see my paperwork and look at the load. I showed him the papers and he looked at them as we walked to the back of the trailer.

"But sir, I see a problem. The delivery address on the papers cannot be right. You have to deliver in a village on the hill, but I think this is wrong. It must mean Perigaux!"

I double checked the paperwork he had in his hands with the invoice addresses. No, it definitely had to go to the village.

He looked worried, and shook my hand.

"Mr English, I wish you good luck!" he said and wandered off, shaking his head…what did he know that I didn't?

The second sign of an answer to the question arrived at a set of traffic lights. The signpost pointed straight ahead for Perigaux, but seemingly straight UP for the village. Do you remember that I mentioned earlier that road maps gave no real indication of altitude? I shrugged. What on earth could go wrong? On the off chance that you ever meet me and hear me say that, please take this as an open invitation to kick me hard in the pants…

I turned left, and the road began to climb. Only, this time, it climbed with feeling. This was a road that meant to touch the heavens and would get there even if it needed ropes and crampons. As it climbed it became more of a track that dodged and wove around the mountain, up through forests. And all the time it got just a little narrower, and narrower, and steeper…

Before long I was in first gear. And getting scared. Looking out of the drivers side window all I could see was down, covered in pine trees. Surely this had to come to an end soon? And then the road was interrupted. A river waterfall torrented down the mountainside, carving a small valley into the rocks. Crossing this was a concrete slab, which was serving as a bridge. It looked as if it had been laid there just temporarily. About forty years ago. The slab was actually narrower than the truck and was just a flat slab of concrete, with no barriers or edges. As I crossed it I could see that the trailer wheels were overhanging the slab on both sides. This was the first time on any driving job where I have actually been shaking with fear. And worse, there was no way back! I couldn't reverse down this track, I had to go on. I decided that when I got back, if I ever survived this, I was going to give Jean-Paul a lesson in early Anglo Saxon that he would never forget!

Finally, after what seemed like hours, and *was* actually hours, I crawled into the delivery location, a small village which was, to be honest, incredibly attractive. Finding the delivery location was simple, as it was the biggest structure in the village, a small printing works. At last. What could go wrong now?

Remember what I said about kicking me?

I drove in to the yard and encountered another minor problem. The rear yard to the factory was actually tiny, only a few feet longer than my truck. And the loading bay was to one side, which meant turning the truck round. As luck would have it there was a small track at the end of the yard, which led in to the forest. I elected to pull the truck up the track and then attempt to swing the back end round on to the loading bay.

I edged the truck up the gravel path until I thought I'd have enough room to turn round and then selected reverse gear. What should have happened then was that the gearbox should have gone **GLONK**, the truck should have shaken very slightly and I should have been able to go backwards. What actually happened was that the gear stick fell off…

I rang Jean-Paul on the truck mobile phone, and before I could say anything he wanted to know if I was alright. He seemed quite concerned. I explained what had happened and I must admit I did perhaps suggest his parents may not have been joined in lawful wedlock, and to my surprise he was very contrite. Apparently he'd told the warehouse chaps that he'd sent me to deliver the load to save them a job, and they'd got quite angry, as this delivery usually went on small vans, as the road was too tricky for even a small truck to attempt. Now he tells me!

He said he'd make arrangements for the Pegaso repair team to sort the truck gearbox, but it would not be until tomorrow, which meant I was stuck in a forest for the night.

I went to the warehouse to tell the crew there what was going on. They were all impressed at having such a truck in their loading bay, and were busy taking pictures! The boss turned up in his very nice BMW to see what the fuss was about and I explained as best I could what the problem was. He seemed quite concerned at my wellbeing and asked if I would be alright sleeping in my cab, or would I prefer to spend the night at his house. I explained to him I would prefer to stay with the truck, as I wanted to be sure of its security and he shrugged and wandered off. One of the forklift drivers nudged me and mentioned his twin eighteen year old daughters. They indicated with their hands the shape of these girls and quite frankly I am amazed they were able to stand up. Darn! Why did they not mention this before I heroically chose to stay in the cab?

Seven o'clock found me tuning the radio to Radio 4, for The Archers. BBC Long Wave transmitted across a lot of France and when Radio 4 is all you can get, then you listen to it, and over the years I had become addicted to The Archers…

The theme tune started, and there I was, in the middle of a forest in the Dordogne, listening to The Archers, just me, the birds, the trees, and 5,000 mosquitoes. So, when someone banged loudly on the door, I could be excused for yelling and jumping nearly out of my skin.

It was the factory owner. He'd gone back to his house and returned with a crate of beer, a plate of sandwiches, cakes and cheese and biscuits. He also invited me to use the phone, but I explained that I had already called Jean-Paul.

'Oh, surely you would like to call your wife?'

He took me in to the office, and pointed at the phone. How bizarre. It was an old Bakelite phone with a dial and it was totally covered in leather! As was a wine bottle, a large diary, a typewriter…in fact a good thirty percent of the stuff in his office was leather bound. He explained that his wife had time on her hands and liked to be creative with leather. He winked, and suggested that her leather skills extended beyond the inanimate, and again suggested he would be happy to allow me to spend the night at his house. I tried to sound casual when I again explained that I would have to remain by the truck, but I think my voice cracked about two syllables in!

Making a splash

As I have mentioned, life can be full of surprises. For me, and on occasions for people who just come along for the ride…

I found myself, one sunny morning, on the outskirts of Paris. On the trailer was a single box, containing a forklift truck, for delivery to Fenwicks in Paris.

Having consulted my A to Z, I found that the street was on the outskirts of the city. This was an advantage, as it meant that I would not be governed by the regulations that ban HGVs from any part of Paris inside the Peripherique ringroad except between the hours of 6 and 8 am.

As a result I was on a narrow road, with an entryway on the left, into quite a pretty courtyard. It was a struggle to get in, but eventually I parked next to the office and wandered in with the paperwork. I was welcomed by a gentleman who spoke American English with a strong French accent, which was slightly disconcerting. He informed me that the crate had to be delivered to the back of the factory, and the loading bay was only accessible from the main road. Having explained that there was no direct access from where I was parked to the loading bay, he offered to send me with one of his men, Pierre, to direct me. It was at this point that the entire job took on a slightly surreal aspect.

Pierre arrived. He was the archetypal Frenchman, as envisaged by cartoons and comedy programmes the world over. He was about five feet tall and plump, wearing a striped shirt, dungarees, a beret, and he was smoking a Gitane. The gentleman explained to him what was required and with a jaunty "Oui, Monsieur" he wandered into the courtyard, opened the cab door and climbed in. After a few seconds he noticed that he was in fact in the driving seat, this being a right hand drive truck, so he shrugged stoically, climbed out again, grinned, wandered round to the passenger seat and got back in. And we set off.

It was an interesting trip. The route took us down narrow, car-clogged streets, through a shopping centre and along winding roads. The journey took a good half hour, but eventually Pierre signalled that I was to stop. On the left was a set of wooden sliding doors, completely blocked by parked cars. Pierre hopped out, and wandered in to a nearby bar. Shortly afterwards several people emerged from the bar and the cars were moved off. The doors were slid aside and I was guided in to a dark dingy loading area. It took several shunts to get the truck facing the right direction and I took the sides of the trailer apart for the box to be unloaded.

A forklift truck putted and popped out from a canvas-covered door, the driver slid the forks under the box, and lifted. The box decided it was quite comfortable where it was, thank you, and so the forklift fell over, quite gracefully. This, it seems, was a problem, because the forklift was not only the largest they had, it was the only one they had...Then someone with more enthusiasm than sense decided to use the overhead crane. Strops were found and the old crane was wheeled into position. I can honestly say that until that moment I had never experienced a true 'heart in your mouth' moment. This may have been due to the 'Max. Weight 10 tonnes' labels on the crane itself or the '22 Tonne' labels on the box, The feeling was not helped by the creaking and groaning of the crane, or the obvious bending of the crane framework. I do know that I made sure I was not anywhere near the truck as the box was cajoled off the trailer and on to the deck.

Finally the operation was completed. The crane was then used to stand the old forklift back on to its wheels and off it putted. I rebuilt the trailer and motioned to Pierre, who had spent the entire operation leaning against a pillar chain-smoking, that it was time to leave.

Pierre nodded, wandered over to the wagon and climbed in. A few seconds later he climbed out, grinning, footled round to the other side of the cab, and got in the passenger seat. The wooden doors were opened and we were confronted by a double row of cars, parked directly across the entrance. Pierre shrugged again and headed for the café bar. I climbed out to watch. A short while later the cars were moved. Pierre ambled back and climbed in to the cab. I waited. A few seconds later he climbed out, grinning, and headed for the passenger seat....

The trip back to the main entrance was fraught with problems. A bus accident at a set of traffic lights meant we were directed through some back streets that were horribly narrow and I really struggled to get through. Pierre sat in the passenger seat, stoically keeping Gitane in business. Eventually we achieved our destination and I pulled the truck up to the office. Pierre decamped and we both went in to the office, where I asked to borrow the phone to call my office for a reload address. The reload was actually from a German registered barge, at a dock on the river Seine. The French American Gentleman had a look at the address, told me it would be a pig of a place to find and suggested that he could lend me Pierre to give directions. Pierre could throw his bicycle on the trailer and make his own way home from the docks. I agreed heartily, as I hated navigating round Paris at rush hour.

Pierre agreed and wandered off to get his bike. Shortly thereafter he returned with a rusty old Raleigh bike with a wicker basket on the front, just exactly the sort of vehicle I expected him to have. We threw it on to the trailer and he got in the cab. A few seconds later he got out, grinning and went to the passenger side....

45 minutes later I drove into a big riverside dock, located the barge from which I was to load and pulled up beside the river. Pierre bid me a fond farewell and before I could stop him, he stepped out of the cab. The drop from the cab into the river could only have been ten

or fifteen feet, but his cry of horror seemed to last an age…the crew of the barge were so busy laughing they had to take three goes at throwing him a lifebuoy.

I was, I have to confess, totally unsurprised that between his lips the Gitane remained alight as he swam for the life preserver. Whilst I was concerned about his wellbeing, having begun to feel quite fondly about him, it did occur to me that he had confirmed my first impressions. He truly was in Seine….

How I broke Bath

I am truly sorry to so many people who may have been caught up in the events recorded below. I'd recently been handed a brand new truck, the first new truck I had ever had, and I loved it. I suppose, in retrospect, I should have realised that it was merely a physical manifestation of Murphy, proving once again that his laws are immutable. Or maybe I am just unlucky...

I am banned from Bath, because I broke it, and a Chief Inspector promised that he would personally shoot me if I ever came back...

It all started in Southampton. I'd made a delivery to a paper mill, and had, for reasons of Commerce, to go to another paper mill in Wales, to load to go to Luxembourg. And I had to be in Wales the next morning.

The route to Wales would be through Ringwood, up through Salisbury, to Bath, up to the M4, over the bridge and away. Only I barely got 200 yards down the road before the truck stopped. This was a bit of a blow. The truck was about a week old, the first twin steer Iveco 400/38 in the country, and as it happened the truck that featured on the cover of that months *Truck* magazine so it Should Not Have Broken.

Iveco dispatched a Grease Monkey...only when he turned up he was more a grease nipple. Honestly, I was surprised his mommy let him out on his own. He had a look and the trouble was that the steel diesel line from the fuel pump to the injector pump was rubbing against the gear linkage. He formed another pipe from steel pipe-stock (bear in mind this was a pipe 3/4" across...the veins in his head were popping as he tried to shape it over his knee...) and then he spliced it in to replace the piece he'd cut out. And off I set.

Bath is a beautiful place. I mean truly breathtaking. The architecture combines so well with the geography. I used to get so...yeah, excited, as I approached along the winding road that leads from Salisbury to Bath, to see the beautiful curved rows of houses and the wonderful villas stacked up on the hills like spectators in a roman amphitheatre. Breathtaking. Although...I did notice a certain lack of traffic behind me...

The route took me through the centre of the city, then over the river, a sharp right turn along the river front for about two miles, then a sharp left and up a looong steep hill, that climbs almost one in three for several miles.

I couldn't help but feel there was something missing from the scene however. There didn't seem to be the usual suicidal car drivers, diving past the truck at the first hint of a patch of straight road longer than their own bonnet, lest they should be inconvenienced. Clearly the people of Bath usually have places to go, people to see. So...where were they?

And then the truck stopped, about 2 miles along the hill climb. Only this time it stopped through lack of traction...which, given that the trailer was empty, should not have happened. I tried with the diff-lock engaged, but it just caused the cab to bounce up and down like a sexually frustrated Slinky, and incidentally spilled my coffee percolator over my sleeping bag...

So, I stopped and got out. And fell over. Bollocks...some idiot had spilt diesel all over....the....road....oh...shit....

A quick look confirmed some idiot had indeed spilt diesel...

So...I called work, who were un-impressed and who called Iveco to tell them to Fix It. And then I called the police.

"Hi, I'm in a lorry which has broken down on the way to the M4"

'Oh, you're the bugger, are you?' which I thought was a bit strong.

For about an hour I sat there. After the first 15 minutes I turned on the radio, for The Archers, and caught the news.

"The city of Bath is almost totally cut off tonight after a truck shed its load of diesel. No traffic is able to move through the centre of the city, as two fire engines which were dispatched to disperse the spillage crashed on the spilt diesel within 100 yards of the fire station. A gritter on the road south of the river also skidded on the diesel and has in turn shed its load of grit, closing the main road to the south of the city. Several cars and at least two motorbikes have been involved in minor collisions"

Oh...crap....

About an hour later, an Iveco Heavy Lifting breakdown truck came down the hill towards me. There was a lay-by just behind me, and he went to turn in there...and just Kept Going. I never saw him again.

Thirty minutes later, an ERF breakdown truck came down the hill, backwards. Seems he'd taken the smart route, and reversed the last mile...

As he got me hitched up and ready to move out of the way, a Chemical Incident fire engine also came down....and also kept going. I never saw him again, either.

And then, the icing on the cake, a police Range Rover. In the passenger seat, a police officer with enough scrambled egg on his hat to feed thirty hungry lads. Clearly this was a man of stature. A man of power. A man of authority. That much gold braid on a cap was not to be found on just a car-park attendant. He stopped just in front of the breakdown wagon and got out, so I walked up to see him. He was going MENTAL! He was arresting me for basically everything from treason to underage drinking. How could I have done so much damage? What sort of person was I to be driving such a dangerous vehicle? So I showed him the repair receipt from that morning, and the engineer in the breakdown truck confirmed that the piece of pipe that the grease nipple had spliced in was not up to the job and that none of this was My Fault. So, I should have been All Right. Except that the scrambled egg officer (apparently a chief inspector) turned to go, stepped in the diesel, and slid on his arse maybe fifty feet...and I just couldn't help myself, I burst out laughing.

Which is why he told me that if ever I set foot in Bath again he would personally have me shot. And why our company insurance broker refused to re-insure us as the claim for this incident was well in excess of £300,000

.

Pig Ignorant

This is yet another occasion when nature raw in tooth and claw is somehow a lot bigger that it appears on TV. David Attenborough, I am sure, never had this kind of trouble!

You may get the impression, whilst reading this, that the job of HGV driver is beset with problems caused by officious Officials, wayward weather, clunky mechanicals and dodgy dealings. This is not so. Sometimes even Mother Nature can be seen having a dig...

I was on one of our regular runs to Hungary and a delivery to Godollo, just outside Budapest. This was never an easy job, as the customs clearance on the Austrian Hungarian border had to be handled delicately. There were certain parts of certain documents that needed to be photocopied and presented in just the right order, or the customs officer would yell a stream of foreign gibberish, throw the paper back at you, wave his hands dismissively and then ignore you. It was then up to you to find a customs agent who was willing to tell you just where you had gone wrong, and repair the problem.

This time however, I was ready. This time I had made notes. All my paperwork was in order. All my 'T forms' were correctly notarised. All my CMR forms were stamped and signed and reflected exactly what I had on the trailer. Even the customs seal numbers were correct on all the papers and signed as such. Nothing at all could ruin my day.

Except the mile long queue going in to the customs park. Oh boy, either the Austrians or the Hungarians were being extra official today. To make life trickier there were new customs buildings going up on the border, for when Hungary joined the EU, and the construction work had reduced an already tiny working area by half. As a result, if any truck needed to be inspected, absolutely everything behind it stopped. And I had just realised. I really wanted a wee wee...

I'd pulled my truck in to the hard shoulder so as to avoid inconveniencing any through traffic and just over the ditch was a fence, and acres and acres of forest. An idea formed. Obviously we were not going to be moving any time soon...

The fence was, when I got up to it, was rather taller than I had realised, but with a bit of an effort I scaled it, and dropped down the other side. A quick nonchalant stroll through the trees, a quiet 'zzzzippp', and oh, sweet relief!

My joy was short lived, however. A **SNORT!** from behind me made me cease what I was doing and very *very* carefully turn my head. Very *very* slowly, so as not to cause offence. The snort had carried overtones of ire, peevishness, and above all, size.

It took a while for my brain to process what I was seeing. I was brought up on a farm. Although we didn't keep pigs, I was well aware of what they looked like. They were muddy, pink, low slung, fatty and cute. Everything, if fact, that the creature behind me wasn't. And yet it was a pig. A boar, in fact. A wild boar, or if not wild then at least a boar that was several stages the wrong side of amiable.

It had tusks that, at this distance, seemed capable of ripping sheet steel. It had teeth that looked as if they could absently chew an arm to pâté with little effort. The hair on its back appeared to be made of Desperate Dan's beard clippings. It stood not in the manner of a domestic pig, all floppy and loose limbed, but in that upright, full-chested pose adopted by Staffordshire Bull Terriers when they are not sure whether to wag their tail at you or playfully remove your leg.

I was non-plussed, which is a polite way of saying that, had I not just emptied my bladder, then I would have just emptied my bladder. I was also in a quandary. I'd had some difficulty scaling the fence on the way in. And now I was going to have to scale it again, but at some speed. I'd heard these boars were no slouch across the ground and here was my chance to see first hand whether the stories were true.

I would like to be able to say that I walked, with dignity, back to the fence. However, as you can probably guess this would be so far from the truth as to be on a different continent. I ran. And…how can I put this? I didn't have time to put away the tool I had been using moments earlier, so the running was both undignified and damned painful.

The short distance I had to cover seemed to be miles, and I could hear the damned animal catching up with every step. Oh, the shame, to be brought down, in a foreign land, in such an undignified way by what was basically 15,000 bacon sandwiches on the hoof!

However, the fence proved less of a problem than I expected. In my, to be blunt, unashamed terror, I almost cleared it without touching it. Although the sharp bits at the top did chafe at parts of me which would, under other circumstances, have been hidden behind several layers of material.

The half tonne barbecue reject tried, and failed, to emulate my flight, and I was so relieved, if you'll pardon the pun, to be on the other side of the fence. I'd made it without too much injury and without being disembowelled by the wretched beast. I'd won!

I turned my back to the road, and made myself presentable, turned back to my truck, and fell, headlong, into the damned ditch. I'm sure I heard the pig laugh.

Cab Boom

There is an old saying. "If it ain't broke, don't fix it" However, all too often people
are of the opinion that if something is old it cannot be efficient. Things that have worked for
decades have to be upgraded to encompass modern technology. They fail to realise that with
the old technology all the bugs have been ironed out. Anything that could go wrong has
already gone wrong and the system has been adapted so that it does not go wrong again. Any
errors have been discovered and eliminated. Any techniques that cause problems have been
adapted until they work smoothly.

Upgrading, then, is basically a way of using the latest technology to introduce new
ways to totally foul up the system...

The steelworks was a vast monument to the age of the railway. Designed when steam
was king, the layout was absolutely perfect for the carriage of raw materials in to the plant,
and for the swift removal of the finished products, to be whisked away across Europe on
railway carriages.

Then the king was beheaded and trucks became the transport *du jour*. Of course,
nobody had considered this when constructing the plant, and as a result loading and
unloading was a nightmare. When carriages are running on rails it is a simple process to get
them into loading bays. You just shove them and in they roll, perfectly aligned with the
loading bays and at exactly the right height.

Articulated trucks don't work that way. They have to be carefully reversed into place,
relying on the skill of the driver to get the trailer into spaces mere inches wider than the
trailer. Of course, truck drivers do this many times a day, so to make it more of a challenge

Murphy had arranged for the interior of the plant to be dark and dull, while the outside of the building was a very light grey. He then positioned them so that they caught full sunlight from about 6am onwards, which meant that the drivers had to try and reverse into a pitch black, curved loading bay, whilst being dazzled by the reflected light.

Having entered the plant, the only way to load the trailers was via an overhead gantry crane. Running on two huge rails, one either side of the warehouse, these goliaths would lift and carry 20 tonne coils of steel over the heads of the workers below, to deposit them in the trailers. This, of course, meant that you had to take the roof off the trailer. We had been issued with curtain-sided trailers which had a clever mechanism built in. If you needed the roof opened all you had to do was release two clips at the rear of the trailer, then go to the front and wind on a crank handle. After about two minutes the frayed end of a steel cable would hit you on the head, and then you had to try and push the roof by hand...

On the fateful day I had reversed in, as usual, and gone to find the foreman to arrange the steel coil I needed. I noticed that I was joined on the loading bay by someone who appeared to be wearing a James Bond style jet pack, with a set of hand controllers. Bemused, I stopped to watch, and it swiftly became apparent that James Bond was actually the crane driver.

It transpired that The Management had decided that rather than have a man sat in splendid isolation in a cabin thirty feet up in the air, it would be more cost effective to have him on the ground, where he could better make use of his time when he wasn't actually operating the crane. It would be fair to say the operator was not a happy bunny. Not only did he have to help out on other jobs now, but he was unhappy with radio control system that now operated his crane. He couldn't put his finger on what was wrong. It just felt...odd.

Now, usually I would take the roof off the trailer, then settle down in the cab, put the coffee maker on, and have a drink and a bite to eat. Generally it would take about 45 minutes to get loaded, which was the equivalent of a legal break. This time, however, I was fascinated by the modern technology, and I wanted to see it in action, so I stood on the loading bay, watching. For some reason I felt like I was watching an accident waiting to happen...

There was no denying the skill of the operator. Swiftly he selected the appropriate steel coil, and manoeuvred the huge steel hook down, and through the hole in the middle. With a *Clunk* he moved the controls to lift the coil.

Clunk again, and the whole crane moved off down the rails, whilst simultaneously slewing the coil across the warehouse so that it would slot neatly into the trailer.

Clunk and the coil moved slightly to the left. Perfectly lined up.

Clunk and the coil raised slightly. Now it was absolutely in line to go through the back of the trailer, and into the well in the bottom of the trailer that was designed to take steel coils.

Clunk ,and this time the only effect seemed to be a look of confusion on the face of the operator.

Clunk ...*Clunk*...*Clunk* .It occurred to me right about then that maybe the coil was going just a little bit fast, and the operator should be slowing it down. I did consider helpfully point this out to him. Then I saw his face and decided that no, this was one of those times when you shut up and said nothing. He seemed to be panicked enough as it was.

Clunk...*Clunk*...*CLUNKCLUNKCLUNK*!

The steel coil went through the back doors of the trailer perfectly. Unfortunately it was not slowing down...

Clunk... *Clunk* ... *Clunk* ... *CRUNCH*

The steel coil went through the front of the trailer perfectly, briefly folding the headboard over onto the cab, before removing the cab of the truck entirely, batting it several feet out of the loading bay door. Then the crane came to the end of the rails and hit the buffer.

The crane stopped and bounced back several feet. The steel coil, however, was hurled off the hook and went out through the steel doors, at a height of about six feet, and travelling at about twenty miles an hour.

I will not, to this day, forget the look on the face of the lorry driver who was standing just outside the door rolling a cigarette as the steel coil passed over his head. The cigarette fell from his lips, and the tobacco from his hand, as the coil continued in its mad rush for freedom, which was brought to an end only when it piled into the side of the truck that had so recently been vacated by cigarette-rolling man.

It does occur to me that on this occasion the act of rolling a cigarette may well have considerably increased the chap's life expectancy, for his cab resembled nothing more than a half empty toothpaste tube.

I looked into the wreckage of my cab, and found my phone…

"Um…boss…got a bit of a problem…."

Gravity Sucks

Over my driving career I have to confess I had more than my fair share of personal injuries, the job can be quite dangerous...

Falling, I mused, is a simple thing to do. So long as you get the start right, then really you have done all you need. The rest is self-perpetuating, and all you have to do is sit back and enjoy it.

Oh, you could, if you wished, vary the experience, but really the outcome would be the same. You could, for example, wave your arms and legs about, or perhaps yell, but apart from possibly changing your angle of descent, and maybe getting a sore throat, the actual act of falling will remain the same.

These thoughts went through my mind as I fell through the air. A short while previously I had been perched on a ladder, trying to get a particularly spiteful sliding roof to actually live up to its name, and slide. A descent from 15 feet should not take any real time at all. However, time fragments when it actually happens to you.

There is, for example, time to take in the scenery. To my left, a large steel rolling mill. To my right, a long warehouse, laden with steel coil. To the front of me is the recalcitrant trailer, whilst behind me a large loading bay. Beneath me...ah yes...

That is the downside of falling, if you will pardon the expression. Falling in and of itself is effortless, and, for the most part painless, unless you should experiment with the limb waving, in which case you are liable to catch yourself on passing scenery. The landing, on the other hand, is going to be brief, messy, painful, and once you have started the descent, inevitable.

Beneath me was a small gap between the loading ramp and the trailer, filled with bits of broken concrete, steel shavings and the bottom half of the aluminium ladder which was the cause of my current predicament. The gap was probably wide enough to take my body, without ripping bits off, but I was none to happy with the less than sterile flooring. However, as I mentioned, I really had no say in the matter, so there was no point in getting melodramatic at the moment. Besides, I was almost at the ground, and so far I was fine…

…and then I hit the floor…

The impact was literally quite stunning. I'm not sure what it was my head hit, but the hard hat you are required to wear in a steel mill didn't really help, as it frizbee'd off, never to be seen again, amongst the huge steel coils.

A digression… the steel coils in this rolling mill weigh up to 22 tonnes, and you are required to wear a hard hat because the coils are transported over your head by gantry cranes. Think about this for a moment. 22 tonnes of steel, enjoying the same liberating freedom I had just enjoyed. Falling and accelerating at 9.8 meters per second per second, until, after four seconds it comes into contact with a hard hat made of plastic, encasing the head of some hapless bystander. Do you think that said steel coil is going to bounce off, leaving the bystander slightly stunned but healthy? Or do you think said bystander is suddenly going to become considerably shorter, with his chin meeting his eyeballs, and his ears in his pockets? Frankly I am of the opinion that the reason they ask you to wear the helmets is that they may preserve the jaw, making identification through dental records easier…But as I say, I digress…

I lay in a heap of concrete and steel, my head spinning, my stomach churning. At some stage I would have to do a limb check, but just for now I was happy to let the birdies and stars circle my head, let my breathing start again, and try and get my heart rate to something like normal. Eventually however, I began to take stock. My ears were ringing, as a result of the blow to the head, but apart from that I didn't appear to be damaged at all. Until I tried to stand up, when, from my point of view, things started to go badly wrong. Sticking out sideways from my leg was half of an aluminium ladder.

I'm not entirely sure of what happened next, but I can recall crawling into the supervisor's office, oozing blood and I can very well remember his response when I told him what had happened.

"You didn't!"

After that, the whole situation took on the aspect of a *Keystone Cops* film.

He phoned the first aid room and eventually got an answer. A short while later a man in ambulance uniform arrived with a canvas stretcher, which he assembled on the floor beside me, and then sort of shuffled me on to it. I could immediately see a problem, as he went to one end to grab the handles, and then realised that there was no one to take the handles at the other end…

He shuffled me off the thing again, and wandered off with it, and returned a short while later with a wheeled chair. Between us we managed to get me on to the chair and he started to wheel me out of the office, until he got to the door and was faced with four concrete steps. By this time I was feeling more than a little light-headed and got out of the chair and hopped down the steps, then got back in to the chair, and was wheeled across the loading bay, to the next set of steps, where the process was repeated, until I was finally located in the site ambulance and taken to the first aid room.

A quick look at the injury made it clear that they were not able to deal with it on site, and so an ambulance was called, and I was ferried to the local hospital. X-rays revealed no broken bones but considerable tissue and muscle damage. I was given pain relief, and the wound was cleaned, internal stitching put in, and it was strapped and bandaged. I was given the choice of staying in the hospital or going back to the steelworks and I opted for the latter.

At the time I was in no pain whatsoever, because the pain relief I had been given was wonderful. I got back to the steelworks and the wonderful people there had loaded the trailer for me, sheeted it and prepared the paperwork. All I had to do was drive it out of the loading bay and park up for the night. I had been advised not to eat anything and to be honest the medication was making me sleepy, so I just lay back on the bunk and...

It was he ringing of the phone at 6am the next day that awoke me.

It was Steve, one of the company directors. He was in a flap, because the steel coil I had on board was urgently needed at the Opel factory in Spain. He needed it at the docks, as soon as possible. Unfortunately by this time the sedation and pain relief had deserted me and I was in no small amount of pain. Steve immediately said he'd arrange for someone to come and get the load, but I volunteered to take the load to Poole docks, just as long as I could take some time off to get my leg sorted once I had done so. Steve informed me that he was now on his way to Barcelona, but he would make sure the transport manager got the message.

It is said that Wales has as much surface area as Texas, but that most of it in the vertical plane. Certainly to drive from Wales to England required navigating over a huge number of hills, and this required an even greater number of gear changes. As I pulled into the port at Poole something in my leg went *SNAP* and a wave of fire tore through me. The muscle tissue in my left leg tore, and that, for seven months, was the end of my trucking career.

Crippling expense

For the first time since I started driving trucks I found myself facing an uncertain future. Trucking was in my blood. I really didn't know what I could do, what I wanted to do, if I could not drive…

The muscles in my leg had been badly torn in the fall and the extra strain of driving the truck had caused all the fibres to separate, which meant that my left leg was pretty much useless. I was ferried home by a chauffer provided by my boss and for three months life consisted of going to see my doctor every day to have large quantities of fluids drained from the injury site, combined with weekly trips to physiotherapy.

The physioterrorist was a grumpy, dumpy, overweight, harried looking Scot, and I liked her. She had the sort of outlook on life that only someone who has suffered much can have, which was strange, because unless she was a very good liar she had been gifted with a sweet life. Yet she bore the look of one who was bowed under the yoke of oppression. The look you see in the eyes of the oxen in India. And she had a terrific sense of humour, which was fortunate in many ways.

"Today we are going to try hydrotherapy!" she proclaimed one morning. I was quite pleased, as I had never had the chance to try a whirlpool bath before and told her so. She looked at me over her severe glasses. "I mean, we're going to see if swimming will help your leg improve!"

I expressed my doubts as to the efficacy of the proposed regime and suggested perhaps some other form of treatment. She bridled. She explained that, as a physioterrorist with many years training and some decades of practice she felt that she was perhaps in a better position to assess whether getting me in a plunge pool would be good for my leg. All I had to do was follow her instructions and I would leave the pool in considerably different condition to how I entered it. I conceded that this would be the case, certainly. However, I also explained that I would find it difficult to follow her instructions, as I would be otherwise occupied. Given that I could not swim a stroke I would be too busy drowning to be able to carry out any of her orders. She considered this, and very reluctantly agreed that any therapeutic benefits to my leg would indeed be negated by the death of the rest of me. We went cycling instead and to this day I have a loathing of those ridiculous exercise cycles. I must have pedalled sufficient miles to see me round the planet at least twice, with resistance settings varying from 'freewheel' to 'there is an elephant sat on your crossbar'. This may also explain why every bike I have had since has had at least 500cc of engine in it.

After three months I was considered well enough to be allowed to have at least a portion of my life back. I was given a walking stick and an orange badge and told to get on with it. 'It', in this case, being very little. Clearly I could not drive a truck, although I managed quite well in my car. Work continued to pay me the bare minimum they were required to pay me, and I just sat at home for another month., Finally I rang one of the directors, and explained that I would have to hand in my notice and look for another job, or go mad with boredom. He expressed surprise, having been under the impression I was unable to do anything and immediately arranged for me to come in to the office to see if I could do any clerical work.

For the next three months I sat in the office, entering data into the computer system, drinking coffee and watching the trucks going past the window. I saw my friends and colleagues as they came in to the office to get instructions, return paperwork or just chew the fat. And I got more and more depressed. The office was warm in all weathers. There were clean toilets, a kitchen, a radio. There was access to a telephone. I didn't have to start work until 9am and by 5pm I was on my way home. I only worked one Saturday morning in four. And I hated it. I didn't 'belong' in an office environment. I was good at the work. I was more than capable of doing the work. Yet I felt I was suffocating. I was being starved of the open road.

Then, one morning, one of the drivers of the truck that was used to shuttle trailers between our Poole depot and the depot in Lichfield managed to stick his car in the ditch, and was subsequently unable to get to work. This left us with a problem, in that the trailer that was currently sitting in our yard with 20 tonnes of *The Complete Works of William Shakespeare* on board had to be in Lichfield for delivery to a warehouse that very afternoon. I asked if I could take it for them.

The manager was worried that I would not be up to the task, but the transport manager pointed out that the trailer was urgently needed, as the books were for distribution to schools for 'O' level English courses, and it was a major contract. In fact there was another trailer waiting in the yard in Lichfield which contained a further 20 tonnes of books, this time *The Poetry of William Wordsworth* that had to come back to Poole for immediate distribution to the schools round Bournemouth. At this, I am afraid I fell about laughing, much to the confusion of the managers. I had to explain that I had to do the job, to see that things went from Bard to Verse. I am of the opinion that they let me go just to get me out of the office.

It would be fair to say I must have presented a peculiar sight when I arrived in Lichfield that afternoon. In a maroon blazer, white shirt and fairly garish tie, grey slacks, walking with the aid of a stick and with a 'disabled' sticker in the screen of the truck. I probably confused a lot of people on the way up, and a fair few in the yard. I was able to get help with the uncoupling of the trailer. More aid was forthcoming with the coupling of the replacement, and I set off back to Bournemouth, convinced that I could do the job again.

Work was less convinced and for the next few weeks I was allowed to take one shuttle truck to Lichfield and back every week. After a few weeks I was able, with care, to couple and uncouple the trailers. Driving was not a difficulty, but getting in and out of the cab was. Finally one of the directors, Steve, suggested that I should be given a warm-up job, ferrying engines and gearboxes for Peugeot from France to the factory in Coventry. The job required no hitching or dropping of the trailers, just backing up to a door where a fork-lift truck would load or unload it. I was more than happy to take this job. I was back doing the job I loved!

For a further three months I drove the roads from Coventry to Metz, hauling gearboxes and engines. It was a nice easy job, and over the weeks and months as my leg grew stronger I came to rely less on the walking stick. As Christmas approached I was asked if I could do the management a favour and deliver a trailer full of disposable nappies to the distribution centre of a national chain of supermarkets. This seemed like an easy job, which would kill a few hours whilst I was waiting for my trailer of car parts to be booked on to the ship for the crossing back to France, so I agreed.

I arrived at the distribution centre well within my booking time and having parked up I jumped out of the cab, which was, in retrospect, not a clever thing to do, and as a result I had to resort to using the walking stick to hobble across the yard and into the delivery office.

'Yeah? What do you want?" a surly voice, issuing from a surly face attached to an overweight body inquired. I explained that I had a delivery of nappies, and Surly explained that I had to tip the trailer myself, using the provided electrically powered pallet trucks. I agreed, and went to leave, when Surly saw the walking stick.

"We don't allow cripples in the warehouse. You can just fuck off, mate!" he yelled. I grinned, and then realised he was serious, so I wandered back to the truck and rang the transport managers, who told me to sit tight and he would call me back. Within ten minutes he had and he informed me that I was to go back in the office and get Surly to sign a *Goods*

Refused notice. I was to make absolutely sure that he signed the section where it said that the refused goods would be returned. It was imperative that I made sure he understood that if they were refused and were found to be not faulty, as ordered, and delivered on time, then the company refusing them would have to pay for the return of the goods. This I did and Surly read the section in question, signed it, grinned and pointed out that as our depot was only two hundred yards down the road from his, the costs were not going to be extortionate. I pointed out that as he had signed the *Goods Refused* notice he then had to phone my transport manager to acknowledge the fact that he had signed the relevant paperwork. This he did, all the time making comments about my limp and my walking stick. He spoke to my manager and said much the same, that he wasn't prepared to let some cripple into his warehouse.

He listened for a few seconds, then said, "Hey, cripple, your boss says you're to limp the goods back to your yard!"

He then listened some more and went pale and started to splutter down the phone. An argument ensued, which culminated with him slamming the phone down, throwing the paperwork at me and telling me to fuck off and never come back. Intrigued, I returned to my truck and rang the office. It seems that I would indeed be returning the goods in question, at the expense of the supermarket. Not, however, to the yard down the road. I would be taking them back to their origin, our depot in southern Italy.

Falling for ewe

The trip to Italy to return the disposable nappies went well. I discovered that I was actually more capable and mobile than I had allowed myself to believe, and could handle a pallet truck sufficiently well to consider going back on general haulage rather than staying on the Peugeot contract. I discussed this with the powers that be in the office. It was decided that I would have to see how I managed with a trailer that would require roping and sheeting, so I was dispatched to a steelworks in Barcelona to load for British Steel in Llanwern...

From Italy to Spain was not a difficult trip. I took in the Italian Alps, the coast of the Mediterranean around Monaco, and down past Perpignan, which is one of my favourite stretches of road for scenery. It had been a few months since I had traveled the route and I enjoyed the sudden flashes of recognition, like seeing an old friend after a long time. Once again over the Poxy Viaduct and into Spain.

I decided that rather than take the motorway, I would drive down the coast road for as far as I was able, just to waste a bit of time and have a look at the scenery. Apart from one annoying incident where a group of youths in a car drove past and threw eggs at the truck, the journey was uneventful, pleasant and relaxing. Finding the steelworks was the work of moments, as steelworks are hard things to hide. I drove in with plenty of time spare and so set about stripping the trailer ready for loading.

For those not in the know, a 'tilt' trailer is very much like an over-engineered frame tent on wheels. With no instructions, no help and a very heavy sheet. The sheet itself is of heavy rubberized cloth, or sometimes reinforced plastic sheeting, cut so that it will drape over the framework to make a box shaped cover. Down one edge of the joins are heavy pressed steel eyelets, which correspond with large steel loops on the other side of the join. When the sheet is in position, these loops and eyes line up. The loops are pushed through the eyes and the result is something like a giant zip. When the whole sheet is fastened, some of the eyelets line up with hoops on the trailer and the same technique fastens the sheet to the trailer. Finally a very long length of steel cable is passed through all the loops and the two ends fastened together with a seal. In theory this makes the trailer tamperproof, as the only way in is through the sheet and the only way to open the sheet is to remove the cable and separate the loops and eyes. Of course, anyone with a knife can cut their own door...

Under the sheet, a framework of steel girders supports hold the 'tent' up. These project up from the floor and at the roof point are met with further girders that run horizontally and fasten in various ways to the uprights. The roof is further strengthened with horizontal steel poles and wooden boards provide further structural integrity between the uprights. The whole system is strong, rigid, very heavy, and to be frank an absolute sod to work with when you are on your own.

To prepare the trailer for loading, you have to do the following. Firstly, you have to remove the steel cable. This is easy when the trailer is new, you just stand at one end of the trailer and pull. The eyelet on the end of the cable just pulls through the loops and out comes the cable. You then repeat this for the next straight run. It does, of course, mean that you have to climb on the roof of the trailer to release the top section of sheet, but you will be spending quite some time up there anyway, so this is good practice.

Skill, athleticism, grace, aptitude, calm, subtleness, a sense of balance. These are all qualities required for the stripping and rebuilding of the tilt trailer. Sadly they are not in my lexicon, so it is perhaps fortunate that the can be replaced by the application of brute force, much swearing and the occasional use of a big hammer. If this fails, there is always a bigger hammer.

Finally will be left with a flat trailer, a pile of girders, poles and wooden boards, bruises, cuts, sweat, and a bit of a temper. At which point the loadmaster will come out and tell you either that you are in the wrong place, and should be at the depot 50 miles away, or that that they 'can't load you today, drive. You'll have to put it back together and come back tomorrow.'

I would guestimate that stripping a trailer in that fashion, on a good day, takes between sixty and ninety minutes, and yet feels like a lifetime. Fortunately tilt trailers are being replaced by curtain-sided trailers, which reduce the time and effort require by a factor of fifty.

Having reduced the trailer to its component parts I waited to be loaded. I was shortly rewarded by the sight of a large steel coil being swung over the heads of the workforce on a crane, and it was deftly maneuvered into place on the trailer. As swiftly as my aching limbs allowed I placed wooden wedges under the coil and nailed them down, then passed two steel chains through the coil and ratcheted them tight in opposite directions, to try to stop the coil moving. The weight of the coil was in the region of twenty tonnes, so if it wanted to move there was little I could do to stop it. The chains and chocks were there to convince it that it was held captive, in the hope that it would accept defeat and not try to escape. Having seen what a twenty tonne coil can do to a cab when it is given free rein I was unwilling to allow it freedom.

If there were a Haynes Manual for tilt trailers, it would probably say 'replacement is the opposite of removal' It is a lie. Rebuilding the Tilt takes even longer, because bits that came out will not go back, will have grown by an inch, been broken in two or got lost. You will struggle and curse, sweat and swear, until finally you are left with a completely rebuilt trailer. And then the loadmaster will come out and say 'Sorry driver, that was the wrong coil. We'll need to swap it for that one' and point to an identical lump of steel.

Of course, the sheet has been exposed to the elements, and is not exactly clean. By this time you will have worked up a bit of a sweat, and the combination means you are a streaky grey colour from head to foot. It is, apparently, a legal requirement that the nearest washing facilities are at least two hours up the road, as this is the minimum length of time required for the sweat and grime to set into an itching, stinking, uncomfortable paste, and almost exactly the length of time it takes for you to become totally homicidal.

Thus it was that when I pulled into the customs facility at La Jonquera I was ready for a shower, a drink, and bed. The showers were out of order.

Three days later I rolled into Llanwern steelworks. I had, by that time, managed to get a shower, and was feeling pleasantly optimistic. I had managed to complete a driving job that was amongst the most physically demanding and I hadn't broken anything. All I had to do was unload the trailer and then I could ring the powers that be in Bournemouth and let them know that I was ready for proper work again. Then the rain started. Being Wales, this was not the sort of rain that falls apologetically, embarrassed about the fact it was making you slightly damp. This was the Vinny Jones of rain. Heavy, powerful, in your face driving rain, propelled with gusto by sudden gusts of strong wind. Oh…good…

Once again I stripped the trailer, the job being made no easier by the wind and rain. Every time I got one edge of the sheet up onto the roof, the wind blew it down again. It took, I think, about three hours to strip the trailer down and I watched enviously as other drivers, with custom made trailers, drove in, wound a handle which winched the whole of the sheet and frame to the front of the trailer, let the crane remove the load, then winched the trailer back into its sheeted configuration. One handed. Whilst drinking coffee. Envy and hate fought for control. And I have to admit that I lost my concentration for a second.

At the side of the trailer park was a field. My struggling had attracted the attention of a herd of sheep. Sheep are not the brightest of animals, but they are amongst the most inquisitive. They stood on the other side of the fence, in a dripping woolly mass of polite stupidity. I was, I think, lucky, because they gave me something soft to land on when the wind caught the sheet and pitched me headlong off the trailer...

++++++++++++++++++++++++++++

I woke up in hospital. I knew, without conscious thought, that it was a hospital. I'd experienced more waking up in hospital than I really wanted, and could recognise the clues. Soft pillows. The distant beep of a monitor. Quiet coughing. The too bright, sterile looking light. The smell of disinfectant that almost but not quite masked the odour of boiled cabbage.

Okay, I was in hospital, check. Next, where did I hurt? On cue, my leg and hips started to throb and grate. Right, leg injury, possibly a fall. So, can I remember where I was, and what I was doing to cause such an injury? Oh yes! I'd been blown off the top of a trailer, at British Steel in Llanwern. In which case this would be the second time I'd been in hospital here, after a fall. Heh, I'd have to be careful, or it would become a habit.

I attracted the attention of a nurse, and after a few minutes we'd negotiated some pain relief, which was indeed a relief, as my leg was beginning to get tediously achy. An injection followed, the pain ebbed, and I lay back on the soft pillows and grinned. I was back in the job I loved, and it felt GOOD!

Acknowledgements:

Two points of view were mooted when I discussed acknowledgements with my friends on Bookarazzi (www.bookarazzi.com). One was that an Acknowledgement should be short and sweet, which makes my life easier. However, the other point of view is that the more people you mention, the more people buy the book. So, I happen to have the telephone directory for Greater London.

Thanks go to Mr A.Aardvark, of....no, maybe not...

My thanks have to go to my brother, my best friend and my role model, who are one and the same person, and his good lady wife, Jackie. A better sister-in-law I could not want.

My sister, Sue, for her strength and support, which I wear whenever the weather gets cold.

A special thanks to Diane Duane and Peter Morwood, who gave me so many pointers and huge laughs and no small quantity of advice and information.

To my friends on the alt.fan.Pratchett IRC channel who were so supportive, helpful and informative. In particular to Suzi, Gid, Cy, Kim and Random for their patience in reading the work and pointing out howlers. These people are nice people, and I am proud and privileged to call them my friends.

To Clare Christian at TFP for having faith in me, and no little patience.

And to my editor, Caroline Smailes, without whose advice, talent, charm, wit and professionalism this book would simply not have happened. It was an honour to have you as editor.

1393127R0

Printed in Great Britain by
Amazon.co.uk, Ltd.,
Marston Gate.